Fodor's POCKET

madrid

D1789425

second edition

Excerpted from *Fodor's Spain*

fodor's travel publications
new york • toronto • london • sydney • auckland
www.fodors.com

contents

maps

on the road
with Fodor's

The more you know before you go, the better your trip will be. Madrid's most fascinating small museum or its best restaurant could be just around the corner from your hotel, but if you don't know it's there, it might as well be across the globe. That's where this guidebook and our Web site, Fodors.com, come in. Our editors work hard to give you useful, on-target information. Their efforts begin with finding the best contributors—people with good judgment and broad travel experience—the people you'd poll for tips yourself if you knew them.

Born and educated in Connecticut, **George Semler** has lived in Spain for the last 30-odd years. He has written for *Forbes*, *Saveur*, the *International Herald Tribune*, and the *Los Angeles Times*, and published walking guides to Madrid and Barcelona.

Don't Forget to Write

Keeping a travel guide fresh and up-to-date is a big job. So we love your feedback—positive and negative—and follow up on all suggestions. Contact the Pocket Madrid editor at editors@fodors.com or c/o Fodor's, 280 Park Avenue, New York, New York 10017. And have a wonderful trip!

Karen Cure
Editorial Director

madrid metro

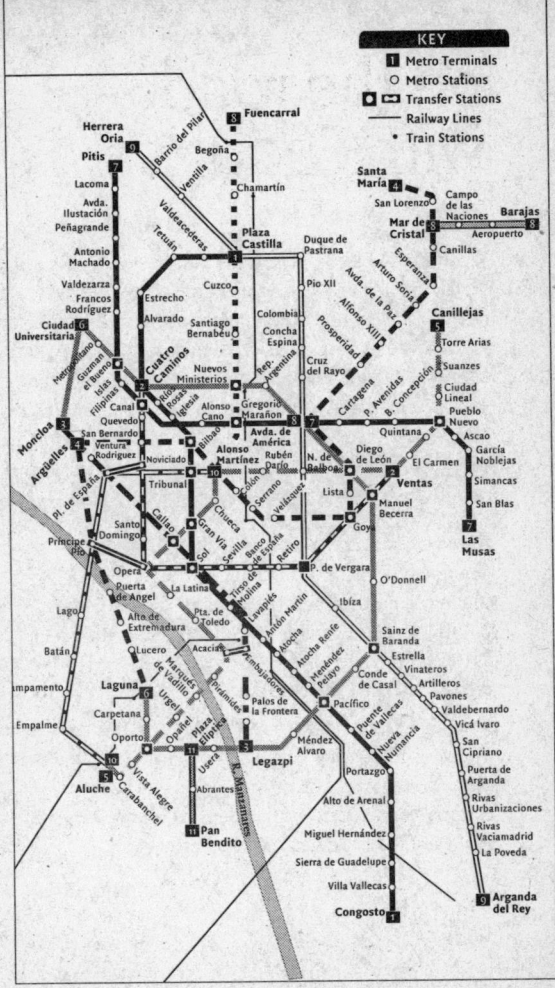

KEY

- **1** Metro Terminals
- ○ Metro Stations
- **◨◨** Transfer Stations
- — Railway Lines
- • Train Stations

spain

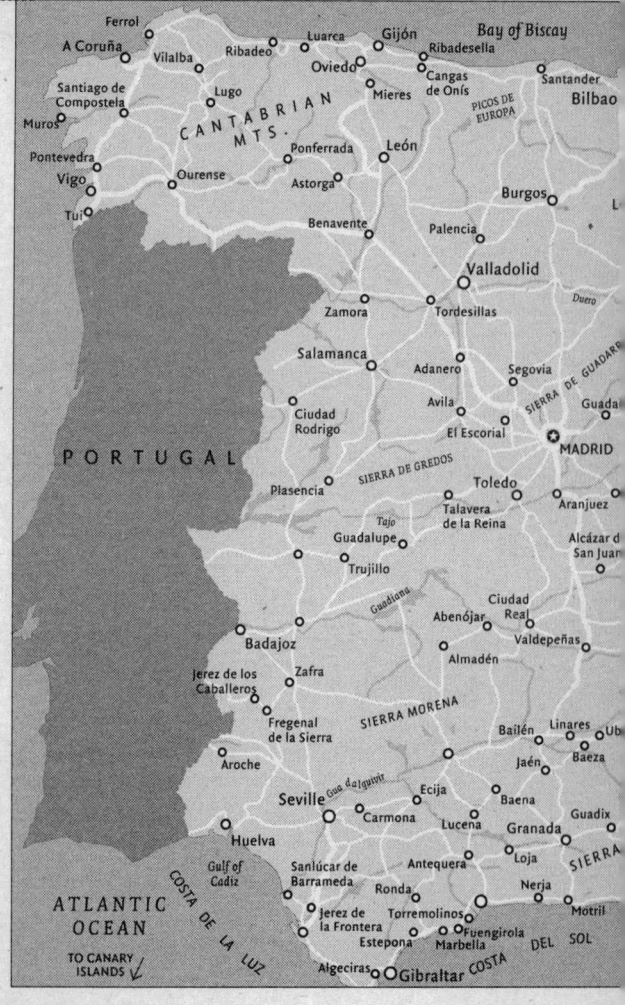

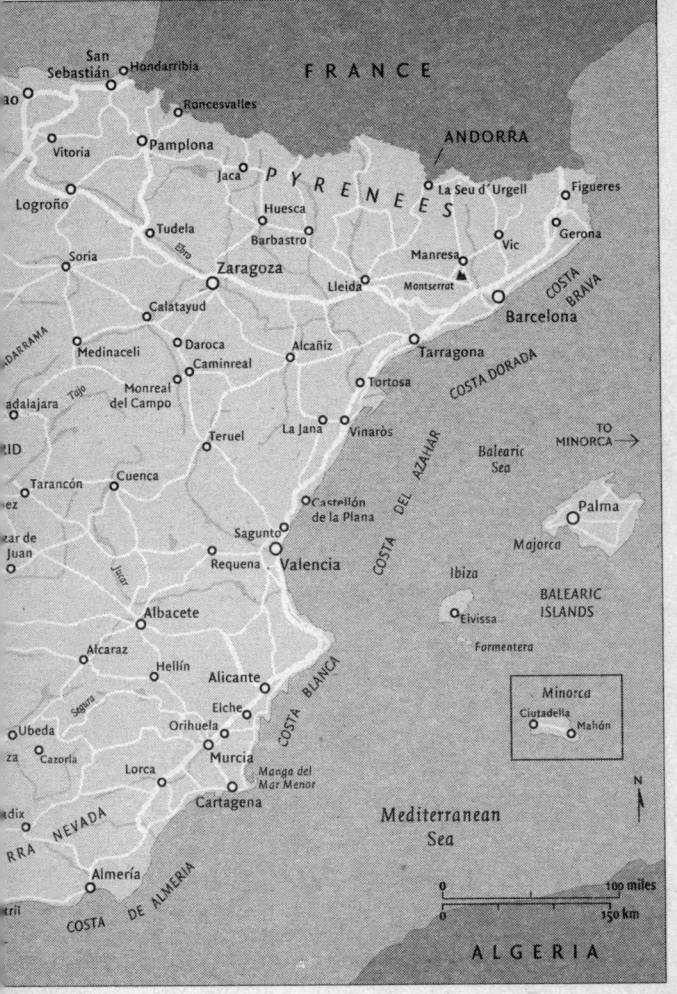

madrid

In This Chapter

Updated by George Semler

introducing madrid

SWASHBUCKLING MADRID CELEBRATES itself and life in general around the clock. After spending much of the 20th century sequestered at the center of a totalitarian regime, Madrid has burst back onto the world stage with an energy and excitement redolent of its 16th-century Golden Age, when painters and playwrights swarmed to the flame of Spain's brilliant royal court. A vibrant crossroads for Iberia's many peoples and cultures, the Spanish capital has an infectious appetite for art, music, and epicurean pleasure.

After the initial gulp of icy mountain air, the next thing likely to strike you here is the vast, blue, cumulus-clouded sky immortalized in the paintings of Velázquez. "De Madrid al cielo" ("from Madrid to heaven") goes the saying, and the heavens seem just overhead here at the center of the 2,120-ft-high Castilian plateau. "High, wide, and handsome" might aptly describe this sprawling conglomeration of predominantly low, red-tile rooftops punctuated by redbrick Mudéjar churches and gray-slate roofs and spires left by the 16th-century Habsburg monarchs who made Madrid the capital of Spain in 1561.

And then are the paintings: rough-and-tumble Madrid's silver lining of color and emotion, the artistic legacy of one of the greatest global empires ever assembled. Having inherited most of Europe by 1506, King Carlos V (1500–58) began to amass art from all corners of his empire, so the early masters of the Flemish, Dutch, Italian, French, German, and Spanish schools found their way into Spain's palaces. The collection was eventually placed in the Prado Museum, part of that monument Madrid built in the 18th century by the Bourbon king Carlos III—known as the Rey-Alcalde, or King-Mayor, for his preoccupation with municipal (rather than global) projects such as the Royal Palace, the Parque del Retiro, and the Paseo del Prado. Between the Prado, the contemporary Reina Sofia museum, the eclectic yet comprehensive Thyssen-Bornemisza collection, and Madrid's smaller artistic repositories—the Real Academia de Bellas Artes de San Fernando, the Convento de las Descalzas Reales, the Sorolla Museum, the Lázaro Galdiano Museum, and still others—there are more paintings in Madrid than anyone can reasonably hope to contemplate in one lifetime.

Modern-day Madrid spreads eastward into the 19th-century grid of the Barrio de Salamanca, and sprawls northward through the neighborhoods of Chamberí and Chamartín. But the Madrid to explore carefully on foot is right in the center: the oldest one, between the Royal Palace and Madrid's midtown forest, the Parque del Buen Retiro. These neighborhoods will introduce to you the city's finest resources—its vivacious people and the electricity they generate, whether at play in bars or at work in the finance, advertising, TV, and film industries, all headquartered here in what Madrid's Oscar Wilde, Ramón Gomez de la Serna, called "la rompeolas de las Españas," the breakwater of Spain's many peoples and cultures.

As the highest capital in Europe, Madrid is hot in summer and freezing cold in winter, with temperate springs and autumns. In winter—when steamy café windows beckon you inside, and the blue skies are particularly bright—Madrid is the next best place to heaven. Moreover, it's ideally placed for getaways to dozens of Castilian hamlets and to Toledo, Segovia, and El Escorial, places cherished by travelers and locals alike.

QUICK TOURS

TOUR ONE

If you have only a day or two, limit yourself to a couple of museums and devote the rest of your time to wandering. See the works of Spain's great masters at the **MUSEO DEL PRADO;** then visit the **PALACIO REAL** for a regal display of art, architecture, and history. The palace tour includes admission to the Royal Library and Royal Armory, both sights in their own right. Stroll from Paseo de la Castellana to Paseo del Prado to see the fountains at **PLAZA COLÓN: FUENTE DE LA CIBELES** and **FUENTE DE NEPTUNO.** Behold the **PUERTA DEL SOL,** then relax at an outdoor café on the **PLAZA MAYOR.** Finally, pop into some of the historic tapas bars along **CAVA DE SAN MIGUEL.**

TOUR TWO

With three or four days you can uncover historic Madrid, visit more museums, and make an excursion outside the city. Follow the two-day plan above; then visit the **CENTRO DE ARTE REINA SOFÍA** and the **MUSEO THYSSEN-BORNEMISZA.** Try not to miss the 16th-century **CONVENTO DE LAS DESCALZAS REALES.** Explore the Mudéjar architecture and flamboyant plateresque decoration of medieval Madrid in the **PLAZA DE LA VILLA** and around the **PLAZA DE LA PAJA.** Venture outside the capital to spend your fourth day at **EL ESCORIAL,** a grand monastery, or **CHINCHÓN,** a true Castillian village.

FESTIVALS AND SEASONAL EVENTS

➤ **DECEMBER: NEW YEAR'S EVE** ticks away at the Puerta del Sol, where crowds gather to eat one grape on each stroke of midnight.

Your checklist for a perfect journey

WAY AHEAD
- Devise a trip budget.
- Write down the five things you want most from this trip. Keep this list handy before and during your trip.
- Make plane or train reservations. Book lodging and rental cars.
- Arrange for pet care.
- Check your passport. Apply for a new one if necessary.
- Photocopy important documents and store in a safe place.

A MONTH BEFORE
- Make restaurant reservations and buy theater and concert tickets. Visit fodors.com for links to local events.
- Familiarize yourself with the local language or lingo.

TWO WEEKS BEFORE
- Replenish your supply of medications.
- Create your itinerary.
- Enjoy a book or movie set in your destination to get you in the mood.

- Develop a packing list. Shop for missing essentials. Repair and launder or dry-clean your clothes.

A WEEK BEFORE
- Stop newspaper deliveries. Pay bills.
- Acquire traveler's checks.
- Stock up on film.
- Label your luggage.
- Finalize your packing list— take less than you think you need.
- Create a toiletries kit filled with travel-size essentials.
- Get lots of sleep. Don't get sick before your trip.

A DAY BEFORE
- Drink plenty of water.
- Check your travel documents.
- Get packing!

DURING YOUR TRIP
- Keep a journal/scrapbook.
- Spend time with locals.
- Take time to explore. Don't plan too much.

➤ **JANUARY: EPIPHANY** (Jan. 6) is a Spanish child's Christmas: youngsters leave their shoes on the doorstep to be filled with gifts from the Three Kings. In many towns the Wise Men arrive the night of January 5 by boat, camel, or car and are featured in parades.

➤ **MAY: SAN ISÍDRO** (May 15) kicks off two weeks of the best bullfighting in Spain.

➤ **JUNE: CORPUS CHRISTI** (June 14) is celebrated with processions.

In This Chapter

Updated by George Semler

here and there

MADRID IS A COMPACT CITY with a rich urban texture. Broad *avenidas*, twisting medieval alleys, stately gardens, and tiny taverns are all jumbled together, creating such a concentration that walking is really the only way to soak it all in. Indeed, walking is the best way to experience those special moments whose images linger—peeking in on a guitar maker at work, or watching a child dip sweet *churros* (deep-fried batter twists, a classic Madrileño snack) into a steamy cup of hot chocolate. Most of the sights you probably want to see are in a downtown area 2½ km (1½ mi) square, from the Royal Palace to the Parque del Retiro and from Plaza de Lavapiés to the Glorieta de Bilbao.

Madrid's greatest daytime attractions are its three world-class art museums: the Prado, the Reina Sofía, and the Thyssen-Bornemisza, all within 1 km (½ mi) of each other along the leafy Paseo del Prado, sometimes called the Paseo del Arte. The Prado houses the world's foremost collections of Goya, El Greco, and Velázquez as well as hundreds of other 14th- to 19th-century masterpieces. The Reina Sofía focuses on modern art, especially Dalí, Miró, and Picasso, whose famous *Guernica* hangs here; it also shows modern Spanish sculptors, such as Eduardo Chillida, and hosts excellent temporary exhibits. The Thyssen-Bornemisza encompasses the entire history of Western art, with particularly good collections of impressionist and German expressionist works.

Madrid's lesser-known museums are intimate and rewarding. The collections in the Convento de Las Descalzas Reales and the

Real Academia de Bellas Artes de San Fernando are superb. The Museo Sorolla displays the paintings of Spain's foremost impressionist painter, Joaquín Sorolla (1863–1923) in his former home, and the Museo Lázaro Galdiano, a 10-minute walk across the Castellana, which has a collection of decorative items and paintings by Goya, Zurbarán, Ribera, Murillo, El Greco, and Hieronymous Bosch's superb *San Juan Bautista*.

Sadly, petty street crime has become a serious problem in Madrid, and tourists are frequent targets. Be on your guard as you wander, and try to blend in: wear dark clothes, keep cameras concealed, and avoid flamboyant map reading. The Japanese Embassy has complained to Madrid authorities that tourists who appear East Asian seem to be at particular risk.

Numbers in the text correspond to numbers in the margin and on the Exploring Madrid map.

OLD MADRID

The narrow streets of old Madrid wind back through the city's history to its beginnings as an Arab fortress. Madrid's historic quarters are not so readily apparent as the ancient neighborhoods of Toledo and Segovia, nor are they so grand. But if you make time to explore their quiet, winding alleys, you'll get an impression of Madrid that's light-years away from today's noisy avenues.

A Good Walk

Start in the **PLAZA MAYOR** ①. Looking up at the playfully erotic mural on the Casa de la Panadería (the Bakery House, named for its former role as Madrid's medieval bread dispensary), exit under the large arch to the far left and walk down Ciudad Rodrigo, then turn left. Across the road is the restored San Miguel market; down **CAVA DE SAN MIGUEL** ② you'll see tapas bars that reach deep into caves under the Plaza Mayor. The entrance to Las Cuevas de Luis Candelas is on the left, by the steps up to the Plaza Mayor. As Cava de San Miguel becomes Calle Cuchilleros, you'll see Botín on the left, Madrid's oldest restaurant and a onetime haunt of Ernest Hemingway. Curvy Cuchilleros was once a moat just outside the city walls.

The plaza with the bright murals at the intersection of Calle Segovia is called **Puerta Cerrada**, or Closed Gate, for the city gate that once stood here. The mural up to the left reads, "Fui sobre agua edificada; mis muros de fuego son" ("I was built on water; my walls are made of fire"), a reference to the city's origins as a fortress with abundant springs and walls of silex, a kind of flint that creates sparks when pieces are struck together. Across the square to the right is Calle del Nuncio, leading to the Palacio de la Nunciatura (Palace of the Nunciat), which once housed the Pope's ambassadors to Spain. The palace isn't open, but you can peek inside the Renaissance garden.

Nuncio widens and on your left at No. 17 is the Taberna de Cien Vinos, a good place to sample Spanish wine. Opposite is the church of San Pedro el Viejo (St. Peter the Elder), one of Madrid's oldest, with a Mudéjar tower. Bear right and enter Príncipe Anglona to enter **PLAZA DE LA PAJA** ③. Down on the right is the ramped Costanilla de San Andrés, which leads to Calle Segovia and a view of the viaduct above. Look down the narrow Calle Príncipe Anglona for a good view of the Mudéjar tower on the church of San Pedro el Viejo, one of the city's oldest. The brick tower is believed to have been built in 1354 following the Christian reconquest of Algeciras, near Gibraltar.

At the top of Plaza de la Paja is the church of San Andrés; past the church, turn right after Plaza de los Carros into Plaza Puerta de Moros, then down Carrera San Francisco to visit the **BASÍLICA DE SAN FRANCISCO EL GRANDE** ④. Backtrack and turn left after San Andrés down Cava Baja—this curving street is packed with bars and restaurants. Casa Lucio, at No. 35, is a favorite of the king; opposite is La Solea, with late-night jazz and flamenco.

La Chata, at No. 24, is a typical Madrid *tasca* (tavern). Continue straight ahead to return to Plaza Mayor.

TIMING

This 90-minute walk requires some short uphill climbs through the winding streets. Allow ample time for stops to absorb the Old World charm—especially in summer, when heat will be a factor.

Sights to See

❹ BASÍLICA DE SAN FRANCISCO EL GRANDE. In 1760, Carlos III built this impressive basilica on the site of a Franciscan convent, allegedly founded by St. Francis of Assisi in 1217. The dome, 108 ft in diameter, is the largest in Spain, even larger than that of St. Paul's in London, where its 19 bells were cast in 1882. The seven main doors were carved of American walnut by Casa Juan Guas. Three chapels adjoin the circular church, the most famous being that of **San Bernardino de Siena**, which contains a Goya masterpiece depicting a preaching San Bernardino. The figure standing on the right, not looking up, is a self-portrait of Goya. The 16th-century Gothic choir stalls came from La Cartuja del Paular, in rural Segovia province. *Pl. de San Francisco, tel.* 91/365–3400. *Free. Tues.–Fri.* 11–12:30 *and* 4–6:30.

★ **❷ CAVA DE SAN MIGUEL.** The narrow, picturesque streets behind the Plaza de la Villa are well worth exploring: from Plaza Mayor, turn onto Plaza de San Miguel, with the glass-and-iron Mercado de San Miguel (St. Michael's Market) on your right. Stroll down Cava de San Miguel past the row of **ancient tapas bars** built right into the retaining wall of the plaza above. Each one specializes in a different food: *Mesón de champiñones* (mushrooms), *Mesón de boquerones* (anchovies), *Mesón de tortilla* (excellent Spanish omelets), and so on. About halfway down the street is the oldest of Madrid's taverns, **Las Cuevas de Luis Candelas**, named for a 19th-century Madrid version of Robin Hood.

NEED A BREAK? The **CAFÉ DEL NUNCIO** (Costanilla del Nuncio s/n), on the corner of Calle Segovia, is a relaxing Old World place for a coffee or beer against a backdrop of classical music.

❸ **PLAZA DE LA PAJA.** Located at the top of the hill, on Costanilla San Andrés, the Plaza de la Paja was the most important square in medieval Madrid. Although a few upscale restaurants have moved in, this little square retains its own atmosphere. The plaza's jewel is the **CAPILLA DEL OBISPO** (Bishop's Chapel), built between 1520 and 1530; this was where peasants deposited their tithes, called *diezmas*—literally, one-tenth of their crop. The stacks of wheat on the chapel's ceramic tiles refer to this tradition. Architecturally, the chapel marks a transition from the blockish Gothic period, which gave the structure its basic shape, to the Renaissance, the source of the decorations. Try to get inside to see the intricately carved polychrome altarpiece by Francisco Giralta, featuring scenes from the life of Christ. Opening hours are erratic; the best time to visit is during mass or on feast days.

The chapel forms part of the complex of the domed church of **SAN ANDRÉS**, built to house the remains of Madrid's male patron saint, San Isidro Labrador. Isidro was a peasant who worked fields belonging to the Vargas family. The 16th-century **VARGAS PALACE** forms the eastern side of the Plaza de la Paja. According to legend, St. Isidro actually worked little but had the best-tended fields thanks to many hours of prayer. When Señor Vargas came out to investigate the phenomenon, Isidro made a spring of sweet water spurt from the ground to quench his master's thirst. Because St. Isidro's power had to do with water, his remains were paraded through the city in times of drought.

❶ **PLAZA MAYOR.** Austere, grand, and often surprisingly quiet compared to the rest of Madrid, this arcaded square has seen it all: autos-da-fé (trials of faith, i.e., public burnings of heretics); the canonization of saints; criminal executions; royal marriages, such as that of Princess María and the King of Hungary in 1629;

bullfights (until 1847); masked balls; fireworks; and all manner of events and celebrations. It still hosts fairs, bazaars, and performances.

Measuring 360 ft by 300 ft, Madrid's Plaza Mayor is one of the largest and grandest public squares in Europe. It was designed by Juan de Herrera, the architect to Felipe II and designer of the El Escorial monastery, northwest of Madrid. Construction of the plaza lasted just two years and was finished in 1620 under Felipe III, whose equestrian statue stands in the center. The inauguration ceremonies included the canonization of four Spanish saints: Teresa of Ávila, Ignatius of Loyola, Isidro (Madrid's male patron saint), and Francis Xavier.

This space was once occupied by a city market, and many of the surrounding streets retain the names of the trades and foodstuffs once headquartered there. Nearby are Calle de Cuchilleros (Knifemakers' Street), Calle de Lechuga (Lettuce Street), Calle de Fresa (Strawberry Street), and Calle de Botoneros (Buttonmakers' Street). The plaza's oldest building is the one with the brightly painted murals and the gray spires, called Casa de la Panadería (the Bakery) in honor of the bread shop on top of which it was built. Opposite is the Casa de la Carnicería (the Butcher Shop), now a police station.

The plaza is closed to motorized traffic, making it a pleasant place to sit at one of the sidewalk cafés, watching alfresco artists, street musicians, and Madrileños from all walks of life. Sunday morning brings a stamp and coin market. Around Christmas the plaza fills with stalls selling trees, ornaments, and nativity scenes, as well as all types of practical jokes and tricks for December 28, *Día de los Inocentes*—a Spanish version of April Fool's Day.

CENTRAL MADRID
The 1-km (½-mi) stretch between the Royal Palace and the Puerta del Sol is loaded with historic sites.

A Good Walk

Begin at the **PUERTA DEL SOL** ⑤, the center of Madrid. If you stand with your back to the clock, Calle Arenal is the second street from the far left leaving the plaza: walk down Arenal and turn right into Plaza Celenque. Up on your left, at the corner with Calle Misericordia, is the **CONVENTO DE LAS DESCALZAS REALES** ⑥. Follow Misericordia and turn left into the charming Plaza de San Martín to return to Calle Arenal. Turn right and walk down to Plaza Isabel II, then cross the plaza to your right and walk to the end of the short Calle de Arrieta, at which point you'll face the **CONVENTO DE LA ENCARNACIÓN** ⑦. Turn left here into Calle Pavia (off Calle San Quintin) and you'll enter the **PLAZA DE ORIENTE** ⑧.

Here you have a choice of going directly to the **PALACIO REAL** ⑨, to your right, or visiting its gardens (1 km [½ mi] farther on) and/or taking a cable-car ride. For the latter, cross Calle Bailén and walk to the right: you'll have a view across the formal **JARDINES SABATINI** ⑩ to the Casa de Campo park and the Guadarrama Mountains. Walk up Bailén, avoiding the overpass, and turn left down Cuesta de San Vicente, then left into Paseo Virgin del Puerto for the entrance to the gardens and the **CAMPO DEL MORO** ⑪. To see the Egyptian **TEMPLO DE DEBOD** ⑫, cross the overpass to Calle Ferraz and follow the Parque del Oeste on the left. Farther along Paseo de Pintor Rosales, in the park, is the **TELEFÉRICO** ⑬ cable car to the Casa de Campo, which grants panoramic views of Madrid. Opposite the Royal Palace on the Plaza de Oriente is the **TEATRO REAL** ⑭. Walking down Bailén with the palace on your right, you can enter its huge courtyard and admire the view from atop the escarpment. Alongside the palace is the **CATÉDRAL DE LA ALMUDENA** ⑮. Walk past the cathedral and turn right onto Calle Mayor: on your left, in Cuesta de la Vega, are the remains of Madrid's **ARAB WALL** ⑯.

Walk back east up Calle Mayor, crossing Bailén. Turn left into Calle San Nicolás to see the church of **SAN NICOLÁS DE LAS**

SERVITAS ⑰. Return to Calle Mayor and press ahead: on your right you'll see the **PLAZA DE LA VILLA** ⑱, with Madrid's city hall on the right. Farther up Mayor, bear right in Plaza Morenas and enter the **PLAZA MAYOR** ① through the arch. The Andalusian Torre de Oro bar on the left displays gory pictures of bullfights—not for the squeamish. On the far side, at No. 33, is the restaurant El Soportal, which gives the plaza's best free tapas with each drink order. (Beware of prices at the other restaurants, especially if you sit outside.) Exit the plaza to the left of El Soportal and head down Calle de Postas and back to the Puerta del Sol. Proceed up the right side of Sol, past the headquarters of the regional government, and if it's chilly consider having a traditional *caldo* (broth) in the charming old shop at the restaurant Lhardy on Carrera de San Jerónimo.

TIMING

Without side trips to the palace gardens or the cable car, you can cover this ground in two hours. Set aside an additional morning or afternoon to visit the Royal Palace.

Sights to See

🔟 **ARAB WALL.** The city of Madrid was founded on Calle Cuesta de la Vega at the ruins of this wall, which protected a fortress built here in the 9th century by Emir Mohammed I. In addition to being an excellent defensive position, the site had plentiful water and was called *Mayrit*, which is Arabic for "water source" and the likely origin of the city's name. All that remains of the *medina*—the old Arab city that formed within the walls of the fortress—is the neighborhood's crazy quilt of streets and plazas, which probably follow the same layout they followed more than 1,100 years ago. The park **EMIR MOHAMMED I**, alongside the wall, hosts concerts and plays in the summer.

🔟 **CAMPO DEL MORO** (Moors' Field). Below the Sabatini Gardens, but accessible only by an entrance on the far side, is the Campo del Moro. Clusters of shady trees, winding paths, and a long lawn leading up to the Royal Palace make for strategically beautiful photographs. Even without considering the riches inside, the palace's immense size (it's twice as large as Buckingham Palace) inspires awe.

⓯ CATÉDRAL DE LA ALMUDENA. The first stone of the cathedral (which adjoins the Royal Palace to the south) was laid in 1883 by King Alfonso XII, and the end result was consecrated by Pope John Paul II in 1993. The building was intended to be Gothic in style, with needles and spires, but as money ran short, the design was simplified by Fernando Chueca Goltia into the more austere classical form you see today. The cathedral houses the remains of Madrid's patron saint, San Isidro (St. Isidore), and a wooden statue of Madrid's female patron saint, the Virgin of Almudena, which is said to have been discovered following the 1085 Christian reconquest of Madrid. Legend has it that a divinely inspired woman named María led authorities to a spot in the old wall of the Alcázar (which in Arabic can also be called *almudeyna*), where the statue was found framed by two lighted candles inside a grain storage vault. That wall is part of the cathedral's foundation. C. Bailén s/n, tel. 91/548–9900. Free. Daily 10–1:30 and 6–7:45.

⓻ CONVENTO DE LA ENCARNACIÓN (Convent of the Incarnation). Once connected to the Royal Palace by an underground passageway, this Augustinian convent was founded in 1611 by the wife of Felipe III. It holds several artistic treasures, but its biggest attraction is its reliquary, which holds among the sacred bones a vial containing the dried blood of St. Pantaleón, which is said to liquefy every year on July 27. The surprisingly ornate church has superb acoustics for medieval and Renaissance choral music; check city listings for concerts. The Descalzas Reales ticket. Plaza de la Encarnación 1, tel. 91/547–0510. 475 ptas. Wed. and Sat. 10:30–2:30 and 4–5:30, Sun. 11–2.

⓺ CONVENTO DE LAS DESCALZAS REALES (Convent of the Royal Discalced, or Barefoot, Nuns). This 16th-century building was restricted for 200 years to women of royal blood. Its plain, brick-

exploring madrid

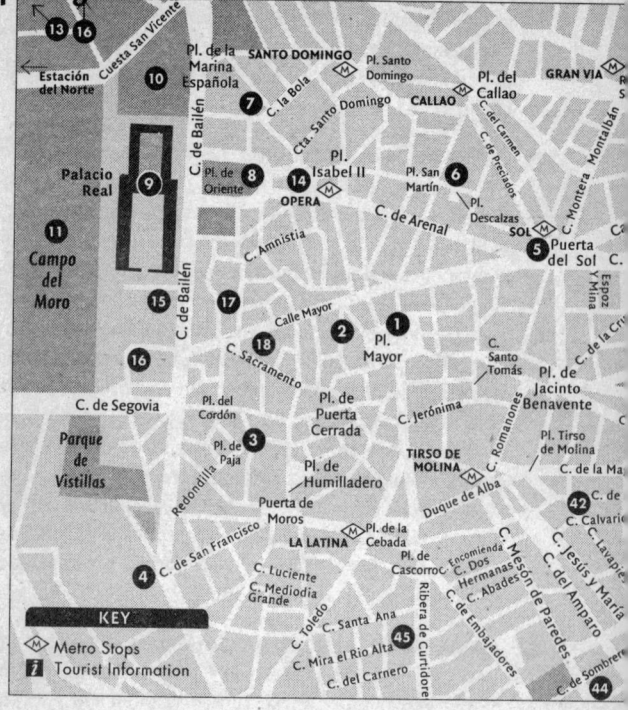

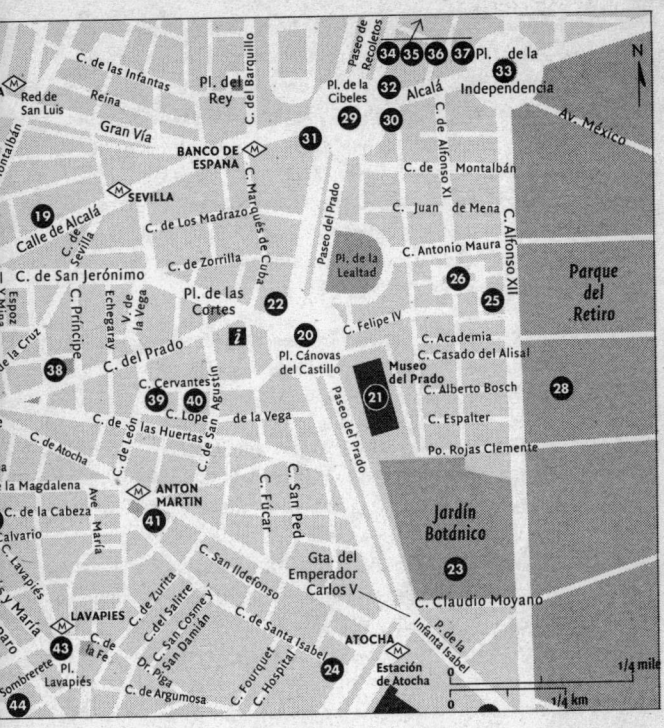

and-stone facade hides a treasure trove, including paintings by Zurbarán, Titian, and Brueghel the Elder, as well as a hall of sumptuous tapestries crafted from drawings by Peter Paul Rubens. The convent was founded in 1559 by Juana of Austria, whose daughter shut herself up here rather than endure marriage to Felipe II. A handful of nuns (not necessarily royal) still live here, cultivating their own vegetables in the convent's garden. The required tour is conducted only in Spanish. *Plaza de las Descalzas Reales 3, tel. 91/521–2779. 800 ptas. Tues.–Thurs. and Sat. 10:30–12:45 and 4–5:45, Fri. 10:30–12:45, Sun. 11–1:45.*

⑩ JARDINES SABATINI (Sabatini Gardens). The formal gardens to the north of the Royal Palace are crawling with stray cats, but they're a pleasant place to rest or watch the sun set.

★ **⑨ PALACIO REAL.** The Royal Palace was commissioned in the early 18th century by the first of Spain's Bourbon rulers, Felipe V, on the same strategic site where Madrid's first Alcázar (Moorish fortress) was built in the 9th. Before you enter, stroll around the graceful **PATIO DE ARMAS** and admire the classical French architecture. King Felipe was obviously inspired by his childhood days at Versailles with his grandfather Louis XIV. Look for the stone statues of Inca prince Atahualpa and Aztec king Montezuma, perhaps the only tributes in Spain to these pre-Columbian American rulers. Notice how the steep bluff drops westward to the Manzanares River—on a clear day, this vantage point also commands a good view of the mountain passes leading into Madrid from Old Castile, and it becomes obvious why the Moors picked this particular spot for a fortress.

Inside, 2,800 rooms compete with each other for over-the-top opulence. A nearly two-hour guided tour in English winds a mile-long path through the palace. Highlights include the **SALÓN DE GASPARINI,** King Carlos III's private apartments, with swirling, inlaid floors and curlicued, ceramic wall and ceiling decoration, all glistening in the light of a 2-ton crystal chandelier; the **SALÓN DEL TRONO,** an exceedingly grand throne room with the royal seats of King Juan Carlos and Queen Sofía; and the **BANQUET HALL,** the palace's largest room, which seats up to 140 people for state dinners. No monarch has lived here since 1931, when Alfonso XIII was hounded out of the country by a populace fed up with centuries of royal oppression. The current king and queen live in the far simpler Zarzuela Palace on the outskirts of Madrid, using this palace only for state functions and official occasions such as the first Middle East peace talks, held here in 1991.

You can also visit the **BIBLIOTECA REAL** (Royal Library), which has a first edition of Cervantes's *Don Quixote*; the **MUSEO DE MÚSICA** (Music Museum), where five stringed instruments by Stradivarius form the world's largest collection; the **ARMERÍA REAL** (Royal Armory), with its vast array of historic suits of armor and some frightening medieval torture implements; and the **REAL OFICINA DE FARMACÍA** (Royal Pharmacy), with an assortment of vials and flasks that were used to mix the king's medicines. *C. Bailén s/n, tel. 91/542–0059. 1,000 ptas., guided tour 1,150 ptas. Tues.–Sat. 9–6 (Oct.–Mar. 9:30–5), Sun. 9–3 (Oct.–Mar. 9:30–2). Closed during official receptions.*

8 PLAZA DE ORIENTE. The stately plaza in front of the Royal Palace is surrounded by massive stone statues of various Spanish monarchs from Ataulfo to Fernando VI. These sculptures were meant to be mounted on the railing on top of the palace, but Queen Isabel of Farnesio, one of the first royals to live in the palace, had them removed because she was afraid their enormous weight would bring the roof down. (Well, that's what she said . . . according to palace insiders, the queen wanted the statues removed because her own likeness had not been placed front and center.) The statue of **KING FELIPE IV** in the plaza's center was the first equestrian bronze ever cast with a rearing horse. The pose comes from a Velázquez painting of the king with which the monarch was so smitten that in 1641 he commissioned an Italian artist, Pietro de Tacca, to turn it into a sculpture. De Tacca enlisted

Galileo's help in configuring the statue's weight so it wouldn't tip over.

In the minds of most Madrileños, the Plaza de Oriente is forever linked with Francisco Franco. The *generalísimo* liked to speak from the roof of the Royal Palace to his thousands of followers as they crammed into the plaza below. Even now, on the November anniversary of Franco's death, the plaza fills with supporters, most of whom are old-timers, though in a few recent years the occasion has drawn swastika-waving skinheads from other European countries in a chilling fascist tribute.

(18) PLAZA DE LA VILLA. Madrid's town council has met in this medieval-looking complex since the Middle Ages, and it's now the city hall. Just two blocks west of the Plaza Mayor on Calle Mayor, it was once called Plaza de San Salvador for a church that used to stand here. The oldest building is the **CASA DE LOS LUJANES,** on the east side—it's the one with the Mudéjar tower. Built as a private home in the late 15th century, the house carries the Lujanes crest over the main doorway. Also on the plaza's east end is the brick-and-stone **CASA DE LA VILLA,** built in 1629, a classic example of Madrid design with its clean lines and spire-topped corner towers. Connected by an overhead walkway, the **CASA DE CISNEROS** was commissioned in 1537 by the nephew of Cardinal Cisneros. It's one of Madrid's rare examples of the flamboyant plateresque style, which has been likened to splashing water— a liquid exuberance wrought in stone. *C. Mayor. Guided tour in Spanish Mon. at 5.*

(5) PUERTA DEL SOL. Always crowded with both people and exhaust fumes, Sol is the nerve center of Madrid's traffic. The city's main subway interchange is below, and buses fan out through the city from here. A brass plaque in the sidewalk on the south side of the plaza marks Kilometer 0, the spot from which all distances in Spain are measured. The restored 1756 French-neoclassical building near the marker now houses the offices of the regional government, but during Franco's reign it was the headquarters of his secret police, and it's still known folklorically as the Casa de los Gritos (House of Screams). Across the square is a bronze statue of Madrid's official symbol, a bear with a madroño (strawberry tree), and a statue of King-Mayor Carlos III on horseback.

⓱ SAN NICOLÁS DE LAS SERVITAS (Church of St. Nicholas of the Servitas). This church tower is one of the oldest buildings in Madrid, and there is some debate over whether it once formed part of an Arab mosque. It was more likely built after the Christian reconquest of Madrid in 1085, but the brickwork and the horseshoe arches are clear evidence that it was crafted by either Moorish workers (Mudéjars) or Spaniards well versed in the style. Inside the church, exhibits detail the Islamic history of early Madrid. *Near Plaza de San Nicolás, tel. 91/559–4064. Donation suggested. Tues.–Sun. 6:30 AM–8:30 PM or by appointment.*

⓮ TEATRO REAL (Royal Theater). Built in 1850, this neoclassical theater was long a cultural center for Madrileño society. A major restoration project has left it replete with golden balconies, plush seats, and state-of-the-art stage equipment for operas and ballets. *Plaza de Isabel II, tel. 91/516–0660, www.teatro-real.com.*

⓭ TELEFÉRICO (cable car). Kids love this cable car, which takes you from just above the Rosaleda gardens in the Parque del Oeste to the center of Casa de Campo. Be warned that the walk from where the cable car drops you off to the zoo and the amusement park is at least 2 km (1 mi), and you'll have to ask directions; it's easier to ride out, turn around, and come back. *Estación Terminal Teleférico, Jardines Rosaleda (at C. Marques de Urquijo), tel. 91/541–7450. 535 ptas. Apr.–Sept., daily noon–sundown; Oct.–Mar., weekends noon–3 and 4–6.*

⓬ TEMPLO DE DEBOD. This authentic 4th-century BC Egyptian temple was donated to Spain in gratitude for its technical assistance with the construction of the Aswan Dam. It's near the site of the former Montaña barracks, where Madrileños bloodily crushed the beginnings of a military uprising in 1936. Hill in

Parque de la Montaña, near Estación del Norte, tel. 91/765–1008. 300 ptas.; free Wed. and Sun. Tues.–Fri. 10–1:30 and 4:30–6 (Apr.–Sept. 4:30–7:45), weekends 10–1:30.

THE ART WALK

Madrid's star cultural attractions are its three superlative art museums, all within walking distance of one another via the Paseo del Prado. The Paseo was designed by King-Mayor Carlos III as a leafy nature walk with glorious fountains and a botanical garden for respite in scorching summers. As you walk east down Carrera de San Jerónimo toward the Paseo del Prado, consider that this was the route followed by Ferdinand and Isabella, the so-called Catholic Monarchs, over 500 years ago toward the church of San Jerónimo el Real.

A Good Walk

Exit the **PUERTA DEL SOL** ⑤ into Calle de Alcalá, and you'll find on your left the **REAL ACADEMIA DE BELLAS ARTES DE SAN FERNANDO** ⑲. Take the next right, past the elegant bank buildings, into Calle Sevilla and turn left at Plaza Canalejas—where La Violeta, at No. 6, sells violet-flavored sweets—into Carrera de San Jerónimo. (If you cross the plaza into Calle Príncipe, you'll reach the Plaza Santa Ana tapas area.) Walk down San Jerónimo to Plaza de las Cortes.

The granite building on the left, its stairs guarded by bronze lions, is the Congreso, lower house of Las Cortes, Spain's parliament. Walk past the landmark Palace Hotel on the right to the **FUENTE DE NEPTUNO** ⑳ in the wide Paseo del Prado—the **MUSEO DEL PRADO** ㉑ is across the boulevard to the right. On your immediate left is the **MUSEO THYSSEN-BORNEMISZA** ㉒, and across the plaza on the left is the elegant Ritz Hotel, alongside the obelisk dedicated to all those who have died for Spain. Here you have a choice: tackle one or both of these enormous museums now, or continue strolling.

Turning right and walking south on Paseo del Prado, you'll see the **JARDÍN BOTÁNICO** ㉓ on the left and eventually the Atocha train station, worth a quick visit for its humid indoor park with tropical trees, benches, paths, and a restaurant. Across the traffic circle, the immense pile of painted tiles and winged statues houses Spain's Ministry of Agriculture. The **CENTRO DE ARTE REINA SOFÍA** ㉔, home to Picasso's *Guernica*, is in the building with the exterior glass elevators, best accessed by walking up Calle Atocha from the station and taking the first left. Retracing your steps to the Fuente de Neptuno, turn right and walk between the Ritz and the Prado. Straight ahead you'll see the **CASÓN DEL BUEN RETIRO** ㉕, on its left the **MUSEO DEL EJÉRCITO** ㉖, and farther on the cloister of the church of **SAN JERÓNIMO EL REAL** ㉗ and the vast **PARQUE DEL RETIRO** ㉘.

Back at the fountain again, turn left and walk up the left side of Paseo del Prado (or, even better, the leafy central promenade) past the Museo Thyssen-Bornemisza to the **PLAZA DE LA CIBELES** ㉙, surrounded by the **PALACIO DE COMUNICACIONES** ㉚, the **BANCO DE ESPAÑA** ㉛, and the **CASA DE AMÉRICA** ㉜. Turn right at Cibeles, walk up Calle Alcalá, and you'll see Madrid's unofficial symbol: the **PUERTA DE ALCALÁ** ㉝, and, again, the Parque del Retiro. About 100 yards north of Cibeles, on the Paseo de Recoletos, you'll see a grand yellow mansion on the right—now a bank headquarters, this was once the home of the Marquis of Salamanca, who at the turn of the 20th century built the exclusive shopping and residential neighborhood (northeast of here) that now bears his name. Continue north for the **MUSEO ARQUEOLÓGICO** ㉞, which adjoins the National Library, and the **PLAZA COLÓN** ㉟. If you're an art buff, press on to the **MUSEO SOROLLA** ㊱ and **MUSEO LÁZARO GALDIANO** ㊲.

TIMING

Including a visit to the Reina Sofía and a turn in the Parque del Retiro, you can make this walk in three to four hours. Set aside a morning or an afternoon *each* for return visits to the Prado and Thyssen-Bornemisza.

Sights to See

③① BANCO DE ESPAÑA. This massive 1884 building, Spain's central bank, takes up an entire block. It is said that the nation's gold reserves are held in great vaults that stretch under the Plaza de Cibeles traffic circle all the way to the fountain. The bank is not open to visitors, but if you can dodge traffic well enough to reach the median strip in front of it, you can take a fine photo of the fountain and the palaces with the Puerta de Alcalá arch in the background.

③② CASA DE AMÉRICA. A cultural center and art gallery focusing on Latin America, the Casa is housed in the allegedly haunted Palacio de Linares, built by a man who made his fortune in the New World and returned to a life of incestuous love and strange deaths. *Paseo Recoletos 2, tel. 91/595–4800. Free. Tues.–Fri. 11–8, Sat. 11–7, Sun. 11–2.*

②⑤ CASÓN DEL BUEN RETIRO. This Prado annex is just a five-minute walk from the museum and is free with a Prado ticket. The building, once a ballroom, and the formal gardens in the Retiro are all that remain of Madrid's second royal complex, which filled the entire neighborhood until the early 19th century. On display are 19th-century Spanish paintings and sculpture, including works by Sorolla and Rusiñol. At press time the complex was scheduled to reopen in late 2001 after a regal restoration, with brand-new halls devoted to 17th- and 19th-century Spanish art. *C. Alfonso XII s/n, tel. 91/330–2867. Tues.–Sat. 9–7, Sun. 9–2.*

★ ②④ CENTRO DE ARTE REINA SOFÍA (Queen Sofia Art Center). Madrid's museum of modern art is housed in a converted hospital whose classical granite austerity is somewhat relieved (or ruined, depending on your point of view) by the playful pair of glass elevator shafts on its facade. The collection focuses on Spain's three great modern masters—Pablo Picasso, Salvador Dalí, and Joan Miró—and has significant contributions from Juan Gris, Jorge Oteiza, Pablo Gargallo, Julio Gonzalez, Eduardo Chillida, and Antoni Tàpies. Take the funky elevator to the second floor to see the heavy hitters, then to the fourth floor for the rest of the permanent collection, which includes both Spanish and international artists. The other floors house traveling exhibits.

The exhibition rooms are numbered 1–45, beginning chronologically with the turn-of-the-20th-century birth of Spain's modern movement on the second floor and continuing to contemporary artists such as Eduardo Chillida in rooms 42 and 43 on the fourth floor. The free English-language guide-booklet is excellent, as are the plastic-covered notes available at each display.

The Reina Sofía's showpiece is Picasso's famous **GUERNICA**, in the center hall on the second floor. Surrounded by studies for its many individual elements, the huge black-and-white canvas depicts the horror of the Nazi Condor Legion's bombing of the ancient Basque town of Guernica in 1937, during the Spanish Civil War. The work—in tone and structure a 20th-century version of Goya's The 3rd of May—is something of a national shrine, as evidenced by the solemnity of Spaniards viewing it. Guernica did not reach Madrid until 1981, as Picasso had stipulated in his will that the painting only return to Spain after democracy was restored.

The room in front of Guernica holds **SURREALIST** works, including six canvases by Miró. Room 10 belongs to Salvador Dalí, featuring the paintings bequeathed to the Spanish government in the artist's will, hung in three ámbitos (areas). The first has the young artist experimenting with different styles, as in his cubist self-portrait and his classical landscape Paisaje de Cadaqués; the second shows the evolving painter of the Buñuel portrait and portraits of the artist's sister; and the third features the full-blown surrealist work for which Dalí is best known, The

Great Masturbator (1929) and *The Enigma of Hitler* (1939), with its broken, dripping telephone.

The rest of the museum is devoted to more recent art, including the massive sculpture *Toki Egin*, by Eduardo Chillida, considered Spain's greatest living sculptor, and five paintings by Barcelona artist Antoni Tàpies, whose works use such materials as wrinkled sheets and straw. *Santa Isabel 52, tel. 91/467–5062. 500 ptas.; free Sat. after 2:30 and all day Sun. Mon. and Wed.–Sat. 10–9, Sun. 10–2:30.*

㉙ **PLAZA DE LA CIBELES.** A tree-lined walkway runs down the center of Paseo del Prado to the Plaza de la Cibeles grand plaza, where the famous Fuente de la Cibeles (Fountain of Cybele) depicts the nature goddess driving a chariot drawn by lions. Even more than the officially designated bear and arbutus tree, this monument, beautifully lighted at night, has come to symbolize Madrid—so much so that during the Civil War, patriotic Madrileños risked life and limb to sandbag it as Nationalist aircraft bombed the city.

⓴ **FUENTE DE NEPTUNO** (Neptune's Fountain). Midway between the Palace and Ritz Hotels in Plaza Canovas del Castillo, this fountain is at the hub of Madrid's Paseo del Arte consisting of the Prado Museum; the Thyssen-Bornemisza Museum, and, five blocks to the south, the Reina Sofía art center. Rallying point for Atlético de Madrid soccer triumphs (counterpoint to Real Madrid's celebrations at the Fuente de la Cibeles up the street), things have been quiet here at the turn of the century, with Atletico deep in second division.

㉓ **JARDÍN BOTÁNICO** (Botanical Garden). Just south of the Prado Museum, the gardens provide a pleasant place to stroll or sit under the trees. True to the wishes of King Carlos III, they hold an array of plants, flowers, and cacti from around the world. *Plaza de Murillo 2, tel. 91/420–3017. 250 ptas. Summer, daily 10–9; winter, daily 10–6.*

34 **MUSEO ARQUEOLÓGICO** (Museum of Archaeology). The museum shares its neoclassical building with the **Biblioteca Nacional** (National Library). The biggest attraction here is a replica of the prehistoric cave paintings in Altamira, Cantabria, located underground in the garden. (Access to the real thing is highly restricted.) Inside the museum, look for *La Dama de Elche*, a bust of a wealthy, 5th-century BC Iberian woman, and notice that her headgear is a rough precursor to the mantillas and hair combs still associated with traditional Spanish dress. The ancient Visigothic votive crowns are another highlight, discovered in 1859 near Toledo and believed to date back to the 8th century. *C. Serrano 13, tel. 91/577–7912. 500 ptas.; free Sat. after 2:30 and all day Sun. Museum Tues.–Sat. 9:30–8:30, Sun. 9:30–2:30; reproduction cave paintings, Tues.–Sat. 11–2:30 and 5:30–6:30, Sun. 11–2:30.*

26 **MUSEO DEL EJÉRCITO** (Army Museum). A real treat for arms-and-armor buffs, this place is right on the museum mile. Among the 27,000 items on view are a sword that allegedly belonged to the Spanish hero El Cid; suits of armor; bizarre-looking pistols with barrels capable of holding scores of bullets; Moorish tents; and a cross carried by Christopher Columbus. It's an unusually entertaining collection. *Mendez Nuñez 1, tel. 91/522–8977. 100 ptas. Tues.–Sun. 10–2.*

★ **21** **MUSEO DEL PRADO** (Prado Museum). When the Prado was commissioned by King-Mayor Carlos III, in 1785, it was meant to be a natural-science museum. The king, remembered as "Madrid's best mayor," wanted the museum, the adjoining botanical gardens, and the elegant Paseo del Prado to serve as a center of scientific enlightenment. By the time the building was completed in 1819, its purpose had changed to exhibiting the art gathered by Spanish royalty since the time of Ferdinand and Isabella. The museum is now adding a massive new wing, designed by Rafael Moneo, that will resurrect long-hidden works by Zurbarán and Pereda and more than double the number of paintings on display from the permanent collection.

Painting is one of Spain's greatest contributions to world culture, and the Prado's jewels are its works by the nation's three great masters: Francisco Goya, Diego Velázquez, and El Greco. The museum also holds masterpieces by Flemish, Dutch, German, French, and Italian artists, collected when their lands were part of the Spanish Empire. The museum benefited greatly from the anticlerical laws of 1836, which forced monasteries, convents, and churches to forfeit many of their artworks for public display.

Enter the Prado via the Goya entrance, with steps opposite the Ritz Hotel, or by the less-crowded Murillo door opposite the Jardín Botánico. The layout varies (grab a floor plan), but the first halls on the left, coming from the Goya entrance (7A to 11 on the second floor, or *planta primera*) are usually devoted to **17TH-CENTURY FLEMISH PAINTERS** including Peter Paul Rubens (1577–1640), Jacob Jordaens (1593–1678), and Antony van Dyck (1599–1641).

Room 12 introduces you to the meticulous brushwork of **VELÁZQUEZ** (1599–1660) in his numerous portraits of kings and queens. Look for the magnificent *Las Hilanderas* (*The Spinners*), evidence of the artist's talent for painting light. The Prado's most famous canvas, Velázquez's *Las Meninas* (*The Maids of Honor*), combines a self-portrait of the artist at work with a mirror reflection of the king and queen in a revolutionary interplay of space and perspectives. Picasso was obsessed with this work and painted several copies of it in his own abstract style, now on display in the Picasso Museum in Barcelona.

The south ends of the second and top floors (*planta primera* and *planta segunda*) are reserved for **GOYA** (1746–1828), whose works span a staggering range of tone, from bucolic to horrific. Among his early masterpieces are portraits of the family of King Carlos IV, for whom he was court painter—one glance at their unflattering and imbecilic expressions, especially in the painting *The Family of Carlos IV*, reveals the loathing Goya developed for these self-indulgent, reactionary rulers. His famous side-by-side canvases, *The Clothed Maja* and *The Nude Maja*, may represent the young duchess of Alba, whom Goya adored and frequently painted. No one knows whether she ever returned his affection. The adjacent rooms house a series of idyllic scenes of Spaniards at play, painted as designs for tapestries.

Goya's paintings took on political purpose starting in 1808, when the population of Madrid rose up against occupying French troops. *The 2nd of May* portrays the insurrection at the Puerta del Sol, and its even more terrifying companion piece, *The 3rd of May*, depicts the nighttime executions of patriots who had rebelled the day before. The garish light effects in this work typify the romantic style, which favors drama over detail, and make it one of the most powerful indictments of violence ever committed to canvas.

Goya's "black paintings" are dark, disturbing works, completed late in his life, that reflect his inner turmoil after losing his hearing and his deep embitterment over the bloody War of Independence. These are copies of the monstrous hallucinatory paintings Goya made with marvelously free brush strokes on the walls of his house by southern Madrid's Manzanares river, popularly known as *La Quinta del Sordo* (the deaf one's villa). Having grown gravely ill in his old age, Goya was deaf, lonely, bitter, and despairing; his terrifying *Saturn Devouring One of his Sons* communicates the ravages of age and time.

Near the Goya entrance, the Prado's ground floor (*planta baja*) is filled with 15th- and 16th-century Flemish paintings, including the bizarre pre-surrealist masterpiece *Garden of Earthly Delights*, by Hieronymous Bosch (c. 1450–1516). Next come Rooms 60A, 61A, and 62A, filled with the passionately spiritual works of **EL GRECO** (Doménikos Theotokópoulos, 1541–1614), the Greek-born artist who lived and worked in Toledo. El Greco is known for his mystical, elongated forms and faces. His style was quite shocking to a public accustomed to strictly representational images; because he wanted his art to provoke emotion, El Greco is sometimes called the world's first "modern" painter. Two of his greatest paintings, The Resurrection and The Adoration of the Shepherds, are on view here. Before you leave, stop in the 14th- to 16th-century Italian rooms to see Titian's Portrait of Emperor Charles V and Raphael's exquisite Portrait of a Cardinal. Paseo del Prado s/n, tel. 91/420–3768, www.museoprado.mcu.es. 500 ptas.; free Sat. after 2:30 and all day Sun. Tues.–Sat. 9–7, Sun. 9–2.

NEED A
BREAK?
LA DOLORES (Plaza de Jesús 4) is an atmospheric old ceramic-tile bar that's the perfect place for a beer or glass of wine and a plate of olives. It's a great alternative to the Prado's basement cafeteria and is just across the Paseo, then one block up on Calle Lope de Vega.

③⑦ MUSEO LÁZARO GALDIANO. A 10-minute walk across the Castellana from the Museo Sorolla, the stately mansion of writer and editor José Lázaro Galdiano (1862–1947) is an abrupt change of pace from the cozy Bohemian intimacy of Sorolla's house. With both decorative items and paintings by Bosch, El Greco, Murillo, and Goya, among others, this is a remarkable collection of five centuries of Spanish, Flemish, English, and Italian art. Bosch's St. John the Baptist and the many Goyas are the stars of the show, with El Greco's San Francisco de Assisi and Zurburán's San Diego de Alcalá close behind. Serrano 122, tel. 91/561–6084. 400 ptas. Daily Tues.–Sun. 10–2.

③⑥ MUSEO SOROLLA. Spain's most famous impressionist painter, Joaquín Sorolla (1863–1923), lived and worked here for most of his life. Entering this diminutive but cozy domain is a little like stepping into a Sorolla painting, as it's filled with the artist's best-known works, most of which shimmer with the bright Mediterranean light and color of his native Valencia. Because the house and garden were also designed by Sorolla, you leave with an impression of the world as seen through this painter's exceptional eye. *General Martinez Campos 37, tel. 91/310–1584. 400ptas. Daily Tues.–Sat. 10–3, Sun. 10–2.*

㉒ MUSEO THYSSEN-BORNEMISZA. Madrid's newest major art center, its spacious galleries washed in salmon pink and filled with natural light, occupies the Villahermosa Palace, finished in 1771. This ambitious collection of 800 paintings brilliantly traces the history of Western art with examples from every important movement, from the 13th-century Italian Gothic through 20th-century American Pop Art.

The works were gathered from the 1920s to the 1980s by Swiss industrialist Baron Hans Heinrich Thyssen-Bornemisza and his father. At the urging of his wife, Carmen Cervera (a former Miss Spain), the baron donated the entire collection to Spain in 1993. Critics have described these paintings as the minor works of major artists and the major works of minor artists, but, be that as it may, the collection traces the development of Western humanism as no other in the world.

One of the high points here is Hans Holbein's *Portrait of Henry VIII* (purchased from the late Princess Diana's grandfather, who used the money to buy a new Bugatti sports car). American artists are also well represented; look for the Gilbert Stuart portrait of George Washington's cook, and note how closely the composition and rendering resemble the artist's famous painting of the Founding Father himself. Two halls are devoted to the Impressionists and post-Impressionists, including many works by Pissarro and a few each by Renoir, Monet, Degas, van Gogh, and Cézanne. Find Pissarro's *Saint-Honoré Street in the Afternoon. Effect of Rain* for a jolt of mortality, or Renoir's *Woman with a Parasol in a Garden* for a sense of bucolic beauty lost. Picasso's *Harlequin with a Mirror* is a self-portrait of a spurned (by Sara Murphy, it is said) lover, while Dalí's *Dream Caused by the Flight of a Bee Around a Pomegranate a Second Before Awakening* will take you back to Hieronymous Bosch's *Garden of Earthly Delights*, 300 yards and half a millennium away in the Prado.

Within 20th-century art, the collection is strong on dynamic and colorful German expressionism, with some soothing works by Georgia O'Keeffe and Andrew Wyeth along with delicious Hoppers, Bacons, Rauschenbergs, and Lichtensteins. Last but not least, the temporary exhibits are often fascinating. *Paseo del Prado 8, tel. 91/369–0151, www.museothyssen.org. 800 ptas. Tues.– Sun. 10–7.*

③⓪ PALACIO DE COMUNICACIONES. This ornate building on the southeast side of Plaza de Cibeles is Madrid's main post office. *Stamps weekdays 9 AM–10 PM, Sat. 9–8, Sun. 10–1; phone, telegrams, and fax weekdays 8 AM–midnight, weekends 8 AM–10 PM.*

★ ☙ ②⑧ PARQUE DEL RETIRO (literally, the Retreat). Once the private playground of royalty, Madrid's crowning park is a vast expanse of green encompassing formal gardens, fountains, lakes, exhibition halls, children's play areas, outdoor cafés, and a **Puppet Theater,** featuring free slapstick routines that even non–Spanish speakers will enjoy. Shows take place on Saturday at 1 and on Sunday at 1, 6, and 7. The park is especially lively on weekends, when it fills with street musicians, jugglers, clowns, gypsy fortune-tellers, and sidewalk painters along with hundreds of Spanish families out for a walk. The park hosts a monthlong book fair in May and occasional flamenco concerts in summer.

From the entrance at the Puerta de Alcalá, head straight toward the center and you'll find the **ESTANQUE** (lake), presided over by a grandiose equestrian statue of King Alfonso XII, erected by his mother. Just behind the lake, north of the statue, is one of the best of the park's many cafés. If you're feeling energetic, you can rent a boat and work up an appetite just rowing around the lake.

The 19th-century **PALACIO DE CRISTAL** (Crystal Palace), southeast of the Estanque, was built to house a collection of exotic plants from the Philippines, a Spanish possession at the time. This airy marvel of steel and glass sits on a base of decorative tile. Next door is a small lake with ducks and swans. At the south end of the park, along the Paseo del Uruguay, is the **ROSALEDA** (rose garden), an English garden bursting with color and heavy with floral scents for most of the summer. West of the Rosaleda, look for a statue called the **ÁNGEL CAÍDO** (Fallen Angel), which Madrileños claim is the only one in the world depicting the prince of darkness before (during, actually) his fall from grace.

㉟ PLAZA COLÓN. This modern plaza is named for Christopher Columbus. A statue of the explorer (identical to one in Barcelona's port) looks west from a high tower in the middle of the square. Beneath the massive plaza is the **CENTRO CULTURAL DE LA VILLA** (tel. 91/575–6080), a new performing-arts facility. Behind Plaza Colón is **CALLE SERRANO,** the city's premier shopping street (think Gucci, Prada, and Loewe). Take a stroll in either direction on Serrano for some window-shopping.

. . . .

NEED A **EL ESPEJO** (Paseo de Recoletos 31) comprises two classy bars
BREAK? near the Plaza Colón—one in a Belle Epoque setting on a side street, the other in a pavilion of glass and wrought iron in the middle of the Paseo de Recoletos. Pull up a chair on the shady terrace or sit in the air-conditioned, stained-glass bar and rest your feet sipping a coffee or a beer.

. . . .

㉝ PUERTA DE ALCALÁ. This triumphal arch was built by Carlos III in 1778 to mark the site of one of the ancient city gates. You can still see the bomb damage inflicted on the arch during the civil war.

⑲ REAL ACADEMIA DE BELLAS ARTES DE SAN FERNANDO (St. Ferdinand Royal Academy of Fine Arts). Designed by Churriguera in the waning Baroque years of the early 18th century, this little-known museum showcases 500 years of Spanish painting, from Ribera and Murillo to Sorolla and Zuloaga. The tapestries along the stairways are stunning. The same building houses the **INSTITUTO DE CALCOGRAFÍA** (Prints Institute), which sells limited-edition prints from original plates engraved by Spanish artists, including Goya. Check listings for classical and contemporary concerts in the small upstairs concert hall. *Alcalá 13, tel. 91/522–0046. 400 ptas.; free Wed. Tues.–Fri. 9:30–7, Sat.–Mon. 9–2:30.*

㉗ SAN JERÓNIMO EL REAL. Ferdinand and Isabella used this church and cloister as a *retiro*, or place of meditation—hence the name of the nearby park. The building was devastated in the Napoléonic Wars, then rebuilt in the late 19th century. *Moreto 4, behind Prado museum, tel. 91/420–3578. Daily 8–1:30 and 5:30–8:30.*

CASTIZO MADRID

The Spanish word *castizo* means "authentic," and *los Madrileños castizos* are the Spanish equivalent of London's cockneys. There are few "sights" in the usual sense on this route; instead, you wander through some of Madrid's most traditional and lively neighborhoods. Within these are a growing number of recent immigrants and the attendant employment problems. Purse-snatching and petty crime are not uncommon, so think twice about this walk if you don't feel streetwise.

A Good Walk

Begin at the **PLAZA SANTA ANA** ㊳, hub of the theater district in the 17th century and now a center of nocturnal activity, not all of it desirable. The dusty plaza is rimmed by a number of notable buildings, including, at the lower end, the Teatro Español. Walk up to the sunny Plaza del Ángel (next to the Reina Victoria hotel) and turn down Calle de Las Huertas, past the ancient olive tree and plant nursery behind the San Sebastián church—once the church cemetery, this was the final resting place for poets such as Lope de Vega and Quevedo. Walk down Huertas to No. 18, Casa Alberto, an ancient (still excellent) bar and restaurant as well as the house where Miguel de Cervantes was living when he finished his last novel, *Viaje al Parnaso*. Continue down to Calle León, named for a lion kept here long ago by a resident Moor. A short walk to your left brings you past the González delicatessen and bar to the corner of Calle Cervantes. As the plaque on the wall overhead attests, the author of *Don Quixote* died on April 23, 1616, in what is now called the **CASA DE CERVANTES**㊉. Down the street, at No. 11, is the **CASA DE LOPE DE VEGA**㊵, where the "Spanish Shakespeare," Fray Felix Lope de Vega Carpio, lived and worked.

A right from Calle Cervantes onto Calle Quevedo takes you past the Basque *sidrería* (ciderhouse) Zerain—where you can catch cider in your glass as it spurts directly from the barrel—down to the corner across from the convent and church of the Trinitarias Descalzas (Discalced, or Barefoot, Trinitarians, a cloistered order of nuns). Miguel de Cervantes is buried inside with his wife and daughter. Turn right on Calle Lope de Vega to return to Calle León, and walk left back to Calle Huertas. One block to the left on Huertas, turn right onto Calle Amor de Dios and walk to its end, at the busy Calle Atocha; across the street you'll see the church of San Nicolás. The predecessor of this plain, modern church was burned in 1936, but the site is historic: like many churches during that turbulent period, the original building fell to the wrath of working-class crowds who felt they were the victims of centuries of clerical oppression. To the left of the church, walk down Pasaje Doré, where, if it's early in the day, you'll pass through the Anton Martín market, a colorful assortment of market stalls typical of most Madrid neighborhoods.

Turn right on Calle Santa Isabel, by the **CINE DORÉ** ㊶, and take your first left on Calle de la Rosa, which after a jog to the right becomes Calle de la Cabeza. You'll pass the restaurant Casa Lastra. On the southwest corner with Calle Lavapiés is the site of the **CÁRCEL DE LA INQUISICIÓN** ㊷. Turn left here: this is the beginning of the Barrio Lavapiés, Madrid's old Judería (Jewish Quarter). Lavapiés remains one of Madrid's most castizo working-class neighborhoods, though gentrification is beginning to creep in; the streets have been recobbled, and lighting improved. Holding your belongings tightly and your camera out of sight, explore side streets off Calle Lavapiés, then continue down and south until you reach the heart of the neighborhood, **PLAZA LAVAPIÉS** ㊸.

Leave the plaza heading west on Calle Sombrerete. After two blocks you'll reach the intersection of Calle Mesón de Paredes, on which corner you'll see a lovingly preserved example of a popular Madrid architecture, the **CORRALA** ㊹. Life in this type of balconied apartment building is very public, with laundry flapping in the breeze, babies crying, and old women gossiping over the railings. Neighbors once shared common kitchen and bath facilities on the patio.

Work your way west, crossing Calle de Embajadores into the neighborhood known as **EL RASTRO** ㊺—a shopper's paradise, with streets of small family stores selling furniture, antiques, and a cornucopia of used junk (some of it greatly overpriced). On Sunday, El Rastro becomes a flea market, and Calle de Ribera de Curtidores, the steep main drag, is closed to traffic and jammed with outdoor booths, shoppers, and pickpockets.

TIMING

Allow at least three hours. The point of this walk is the general atmosphere. The Anton Martín market comes to life every weekday morning, while the streets surrounding the Plaza Santa Ana are more interesting after dark, as they pack some of Madrid's best tapas bars and nightspots. El Rastro can be saved for a Sunday morning if you decide to join the milling throng at the flea market.

Sights to See

BARRIO LAVAPIÉS. The Barrio Lavapiés is Madrid's old Judería. Like Moors, Jews were forced to live outside the city walls after the Christian reconquest hit Madrid in 1085, and this was one of the suburbs they founded. Known as Lavapiés (literally "washfeet") after the medieval custom of bathing one's feet before entering the *aljama* (ghetto), this hillside neighborhood is today a quintessentially grass-roots working-class Madrid barrio, rife with artists, students, and aspiring actors. Be on your guard for pickpockets, and turn back if you don't feel safe.

42 CÁRCEL DE LA INQUISICIÓN (Inquisition Jail). Unmarked by any historical plaque, the former jail at the southeast corner of Calle Cabeza and Calle Lavapiés is now a large tapas bar, the **TABERNA DEL AVAPIÉS,** named for the old Jewish quarter. Here Jews, Moors, and others designated unrepentant heathens or sinners bent to the inquisitors' whims; the prison later became a Cárcel de la Corona (Crown Prison) for the incarceration of wayward soldiers, priests, and nuns. Ask a bartender if you can see the original, two-story medieval patio out back—it's tiny, but highly evocative.

39 CASA DE CERVANTES. A plaque marks the private home where Miguel de Cervantes Saavedra, author of *Don Quixote de la Mancha*, committed his final words to paper: "Puesto ya el pie en el estribo, con ansias de la muerte . . ." ("One foot already in the stirrup and yearning for death . . ."). The Western world's first runaway bestseller, and still one of the most widely translated and read books in the world, Cervantes' spoof of a knightly novel playfully but profoundly satirized Spain's rise and decline while portraying man's dual nature in the pragmatic Sancho Panza and the idealistic Don Quixote, ever in search of wrongs to right. *C. Cervantes and C. León.*

40 CASA DE LOPE DE VEGA. Considered the Shakespeare of Spanish literature, Fray Felix Lope de Vega Carpio (1562–1635), a contemporary and adversary of Cervantes, wrote some 1,800 plays and enjoyed great success during his lifetime. His former home is now a museum with period furnishings, offering an intimate look into a bygone era: everything here, from the whale-oil lamps and candles to the well in the tiny garden and the pans used to warm the bedsheets, brings you closer to the great dramatist. Don't miss the Latin inscription over the door: PARVA PROPIA MAGNA / MAGNA ALIENA PARVA (small but mine big / big but someone else's small). C. Cervantes 11, tel. 91/429–9216. 200 ptas. Sept.–July, weekdays 9:30–2, Sat. 10–2.

NEED A BREAK? **TABERNA DE ANTONIO SÁNCHEZ** – Drop into Madrid's oldest tavern for a glass of wine and some tapas, or just a peek. The dark walls (lined with bullfighting paintings), zinc bar, and pulley system used to lift casks of wine from the cellar look much the same as they did when the place first opened in 1830. Meals are also served in a dining room in the back. Specialties include *rabo de buey* (bull's-tail stew) and *morcillo al horno* (a beef stew). *Mesón de Paredes 13.*

41 **CINE DORÉ.** A rare example of Art Nouveau architecture in Madrid, the hip Cine Doré shows movies from the Spanish National Film Archives and eclectic foreign films. Show times are listed in newspapers under FILMOTECA. The lobby, trimmed with smart pink neon, has a sleek café-bar and a good bookshop. *C. Santa Isabel 3, tel. 91/369–1125. Tues.–Sun.; hrs vary depending on show times.*

44 **CORRALA.** This structure is not unlike the *corrales* that were used as Madrid's early theaters; there's even a plaque here to remind you that the setting for the famous 19th-century *zarzuela* (light opera) *La Revoltosa* was a *corrala* like this one. City-sponsored musical-theater events are occasionally held here in summer. The ruins across the street were once the **ESCOLAPÍOS DE SAN FERNANDO,** one of several churches and parochial schools that fell victim to anti-Catholic sentiments during the Civil War. *C. Mesón de Paredes and C. Sombrerete.*

45 **EL RASTRO.** Named for the *arrastre* (dragging) of animals in and out of the slaughterhouse that once stood here, and specifically, the *rastro* (blood trail) left behind, this site explodes into a rollicking flea market every Sunday morning from 10 to 2. For serious browsing and bargaining, any *other* morning is a better time to turn up treasures such as old iron grillwork, a marble tabletop, or a gilt picture frame, but Sundays bring out a range of truly bizarre bric-a-brac ranging from stolen earrings to sent postcards to thrown-out love letters. Even so, people-watching is the best part.

㊸ PLAZA LAVAPIÉS. The heart of the historic Jewish *barrio*, this picturesque plaza remains a neighborhood hub. To the left is the Calle de la Fe (Street of Faith), which was called Calle Sinagoga until the expulsion of the Jews in 1492. The church of **SAN LORENZO** at the end was built on the site of the razed synagogue. Legend has it that Jews and Moors who chose baptism over exile were forced to walk up this street barefoot to the ceremony to demonstrate the sincerity of their new faith. *Top of C. de la Fe.*

㊳ PLAZA SANTA ANA. This plaza was the heart of the theater district in the 17th century—the golden age of Spanish literature—and is now the center of Madrid's thumping nightlife. A statue of 17th-century playwright Pedro Calderón de la Barca faces the **TEATRO ESPAÑOL.** Inscribed with the names of Spain's greatest dramatists and rebuilt in 1980 following a fire, the theater stands on the site where plays were performed as early as the 16th century in a rowdy outdoor setting called a *corrala*. These makeshift theaters were usually installed in a vacant lot between two apartment buildings, and families with balconies overlooking the action rented out seats to wealthy patrons of the arts. Opposite the theater, the **CASA DE GUADALAJARA,** with a facade of ceramic tile, is currently a popular nightspot. The **GRAN HOTEL REINA VICTORIA** was not always so upscale but has always been favored by bullfighters, including Manolete. Off to the side of the hotel is the diminutive **PLAZA DEL ÁNGEL,** home to one of Madrid's best jazz clubs, the Café Central. Back on Plaza Santa Ana is one of Madrid's most famous cafés, the former Hemingway hangout **CERVECERÍA ALEMANA,** still catnip to writers, poets, and beer drinkers.

In This Chapter

Updated by George Semler

eating out

MADRID HAS ATTRACTED GENERATIONS of courtiers, diplomats, and tradesmen, all of whom have brought culinary tastes and styles from other parts of the world. The city's best restaurants specialize in Basque cooking, Spain's haute cuisine, and numerous seafood houses, take full advantage of the abundant fish trucked in nightly from the Atlantic and the Mediterranean coasts.

Madrid's own cuisine is based on the roasts and thick soups and stews of Castile, Spain's high central *meseta* (plain). Roast suckling pig and lamb are standard Madrid feasts, as are baby goat and chunks of beef from Ávila. *Cocido madrileño* (garbanzo-bean stew) and *callos a la madrileña* (stewed tripe) are fundamental local specialties. Cocido is a delicious and hearty winter meal consisting of garbanzo beans, vegetables, potatoes, sausages, and pork. The best cocidos are slowly simmered in earthenware crocks over open fires and served as a complete meal in several courses. You can order cocido in the most elegant restaurants as well as the humblest holes-in-the-wall, and it's usually offered as a midday selection on Monday or Wednesday. Callos are a much simpler concoction of veal tripe stewed with tomatoes, onions, hot paprika, and garlic. *Jamón serrano* (cured ham)—a specialty from the livestock lands of Teruel, Extremadura, and Andalusia—has become a staple in Madrid; wanderers are likely to come across a *museo del jamón* (literally, ham museum), where endless legs of the dried delicacy dangle in store windows or in bars. Restaurant windows betray a local affinity for pork products in general, particularly hams and baby suckling pigs. As for fast food, busy Madrileños grab a *bocadillo* (sandwich) from a stand for a quick bite.

The house wine in most basic Madrid restaurants is a sturdy, uncomplicated Valdepeñas from La Mancha. Serious dining is normally accompanied by a good Rioja or a more complex Ribera de Duero, the latter from northern Castile. A traditional, anise-flavored liqueur (*anís*) is produced outside the village of Chinchón.

PRICES AND DRESS

Dress in most Madrid restaurants and tapas bars is casual but stylish. Compared with Barcelona, the pricier places are a bit more formal; men often wear jackets and ties, and women often wear skirts.

CATEGORY	COST*
$$$$	over 4,000 ptas./€24
$$$	3,000 ptas.–4,000 ptas./€18–€24
$$	2,000 ptas.–3,000 ptas./€12–€18
$	under 2,000 ptas./€12

*per person for a main course at dinner

HOW AND WHEN

Most restaurants don't serve breakfast (*desayuno*); for coffee and carbohydrates, head to a bar or *cafetería*. Outside major hotels, which serve buffet breakfasts, breakfast in Spain is usually limited to coffee and toast or a roll. Lunch (*comida* or *almuerzo*) traditionally consists of an appetizer, a main course, and dessert, followed by coffee and perhaps a liqueur. Between lunch and dinner the best way to snack is to sample some *tapas* (appetizers) at a bar; normally you can choose from quite a variety. Dinner (*cena*) is somewhat lighter, with perhaps only one course.

In addition to an à la carte menu, most restaurants offer a daily fixed-price menu (*menú del día*) consisting of two courses, coffee, and dessert at a very attractive price. If the server does not suggest the menú del día when you're seated (perhaps on the assumption that foreigners will order à la carte), feel free to ask for it—"Hay menú del día, por favor?"

Madrileños tend to eat their meals even later than other Spaniards, and that's saying something. Restaurants generally open for lunch at 1:30 and fill up by 3. Dinnertime begins at 9, but reservations for 11 are common, and a meal can be a wonderfully lengthy (up to three hours) affair. Restaurants perform equally well at lunchtime, when most places offer a menú del día, which includes a main course, wine, dessert, wine, and coffee. If you're not a night owl, make the most of the early evening tapas hour and try to defy your body clock for at least one night: a late dinner here is the only kind.

Credit cards are widely accepted in Spanish restaurants. If you pay by credit card, leave the tip in cash.

$$$$ HORCHER. Once considered the finest in Madrid, this classic restaurant at the edge of the Parque del Retiro is now an overpriced monument to its former glory. Specialties include the kinds of game dishes traditionally favored by Spanish aristocracy: wild boar, venison, roast duck. The star appetizer is lobster salad with truffles. Dishes like Stroganoff with mustard, pork chops with sauerkraut, and *baumkuchen* (a chocolate-covered fruit and cake dessert) reflect the restaurant's Germanic roots (The Horcher family had a restaurant in Berlin at the turn of the 20th century). The intimate dining room is decorated with rust-colored brocade and antique Austrian porcelain, and a wide selection of French and German wines rounds out the menu. Jacket and tie are required. *Alfonso XII 6, tel. 91/522–0731. Reservations essential. AE, DC, MC, V. Closed Sun. and Aug. No lunch Sat.*

$$$$ LA BROCHE. Sergi Arola, who trained with celebrity chef Ferrán ★ Adriá, has added his own twists and innovations to those of the

Catalan master and vaulted directly to the top of Madrid's dining charts. The minimalist dining room, all clean white surfaces and soft yet abundant light, clears the decks for maximum taste-bud protagonism, and indeed you'll need to concentrate on the hot-cold, surf-turf counterpoints of your codfish soup with bacon ice cream or marinated sardine with herring roe. Opt for the *menú de degustación* and let Sergi and his staff run you through the gastronomic color wheel, generally progressing from light to dark, fish to foie, seafood to tenderloin. The wine list is superb; try a peppery Priorat (a Miserere, for example) with your beef or venison. The restaurant's name comes from the expression *broche de oro* (literally, "brooch of gold"), meaning the finishing touch of perfection. *Miguel Angel 29, tel. 91/399-3778. Reservations essential. AE, DC, MC, V. Closed Sun. and Easter wk. No lunch Sat.*

$$$$ **LA TERRAZA—CASINO DE MADRID.** This rooftop terrace just
★ off Puerta del Sol offers a glimpse of the deluxe interior of one of Madrid's oldest, most exclusive clubs (the *casino* was a club for gentlemen, not gamblers). The culinary inventions are inspired and overseen by Ferrán Adriá, one of the hottest chefs in Europe. Adriá is not present—he runs his own famous restaurant, El Bullí, near Roses in Catalonia—but his ideas are. Francisco Roncero's creations closely follow Adriá's trademarks: the lightest and tastiest of mousses and foams, ravioli in rare flavors that explode in the mouth, *crustaceos en suquet con alcachofas y patatas* (crustaceans in their juices with artichokes and potatoes). For the full gamut of epicurean titillation, splurge on the 11-plate tasting menu, 10,000 ptas. per gastronome. On warm evenings the terrace is stunning. *Alcalá 15, tel. 91/521-8700. Reservations essential. AE, DC, MC, V. Closed Sun. and Aug. No lunch Sat.*

$$$$ **LHARDY.** Serving Madrid specialties in the same central location for more than 150 years, Lhardy looks pretty much the same as it must have on day one, with its dark-wood paneling, brass chandeliers, and red-velvet chairs. The menu offers international fare, but most diners come for the traditional cocido a la madrileña

and callos a la madrileña. Game, sea bass in champagne sauce, and dessert soufflés are also finely prepared. The dining rooms are upstairs; the ground-floor entry doubles as a delicatessen and stand-up coffee bar that fills on chilly winter mornings with shivering souls sipping steaming-hot *caldo* (chicken broth) from silver urns. *Carrera de San Jerónimo 8, tel. 91/522–2207. AE, DC, MC, V. Closed Aug. No dinner Sun.*

$$$$ **ZALACAÍN.** A deep-apricot color scheme, set off by dark wood and
★ gleaming silver, makes this restaurant look like an exclusive villa. Zalacaín introduced nouvelle cuisine to Spain in the 1970s and is now something of a classic. Splurge on dishes like prawn salad in avocado vinaigrette, lobster salad in an emulsion of virgin olive oil and sherry vinegar, and roast pheasant with truffles; or sample the chef's own choices with a tasting menu. Service is somewhat stuffy, and jackets are required. *Alvarez de Baena 4, tel. 91/561–4840. Reservations essential. AE, DC, V. Closed Sun., Aug., and Easter Week. No lunch Sat.*

$$$–$$$$ **LA TRAINERA.** With its nautical decor and maze of little dining rooms, this informal restaurant is all about fresh seafood—the best money can buy. Crab, lobster, shrimp, mussels, and a dozen other types of shellfish are served by weight in *raciones* (large portions). Although many Spanish diners share several plates of these shellfish as their entire meal, the grilled hake, sole, or turbot makes an unbeatable second course. To accompany the legendary *carabineros* (giant scarlet shrimp), skip the listless house wine and go for a bottle of Albariño, from the southern Galician coast. *Lagasca 60, tel. 91/576–8035. AE, MC, V. Closed Sun. and Aug.*

$$$–$$$$ **PEDRO LARUMBE.** This excellent restaurant is literally the pinnacle of the ABC shopping center between Paseo de la Castellana and Calle Serrano. Dining quarters include a lovely summer roof terrace, which is glassed in for the winter, and an Andalusian patio. Chef-owner Pedro Larumbe is known for his presentations of such contemporary dishes as *cazuela de cocochas con patatas al*

pil-pil (a casserole of tender cheeks of hake, cooked in their own juices combined with oil and garlic, and served with potatoes). There's a salad bar at lunchtime, and the dessert buffet is an art exhibit. Good wine list. *Paseo de la Castellana 34/C. Serrano 61, tel. 91/575–1112. AE, DC, MC, V. Closed Sun., Easter wk, and 2 wks in Aug. No lunch Sat.*

$$$–$$$$ VIRIDIANA. Viridiana has a relaxed, somewhat cramped bistro atmosphere, its black-and-white decor punctuated by prints from Luis Buñuel's classic anticlerical film (for which the place is named). Iconoclast chef Abraham Garcia says "market-based" is too narrow a description for his creative menu, which changes every two weeks depending on what's in season. You might find red onions stuffed with *morcilla* (black pudding); soft flour tortillas wrapped around marinated fresh tuna; or filet mignon in white truffle sauce. If it's available, try the superb duck pâté drizzled with sherry and served with Sauternes or Tokay wine. The tangy grapefruit sherbet is a marvel. *Juan de Mena 14, tel. 91/531–5222. Reservations essential. AE, DC, MC, V. Closed Sun. and Holy Week.*

$$$ ASADOR FRONTÓN. This popular, long-established Basque restaurant serves outstanding meat and fish. It has a few satellites now, but the original is more old-fashioned, and still has a jolly waitstaff—unusual in Spain. Appetizers include *anchoa fresca* (fresh grilled anchovies) and *pimientos rellenos con bacalao* (peppers stuffed with cod). The huge, delicious *chuleton* (T-bone steak), seared on a charcoal grill and lightly sprinkled with sea salt, is for two or more; order *cogollo de lechuga* (lettuce hearts) or another vegetable to accompany. The tender *cocochas de merluza* (hake morsels in green parsley sauce) are deliciously light. *Tirso de Molina 7 (upstairs at back), tel. 91/369–1617. Reservations essential. AE, DC, MC, V. No dinner Sun.*

$$$ CASA BENIGNO. A specialist in Mediterranean cuisine, this intimate hideaway in northeastern Madrid is best known for its rice dishes, including *arroz a banda* (rice with seafood) and the best paella in town. King Juan Carlos is a regular. Accompany the culinary inventions with your choice of olive oil from a truly encyclopedic selection. Owner-creator Don Norberto takes gracious care of international guests, suggesting unusual wines from all over the Iberian Peninsula and guiding you congenially through the casual, understated premises. *Benigno Soto 9, tel. 91/ 416–9357. Reservations essential. AE, DC, MC, V. Closed Aug., Holy Week, and Christmas wk. No dinner Sun.*

$$$ EL BORBOLLÓN. For nearly two decades the friendly Castro family has run this elegant yet comfortable restaurant and bar between Paseo de Recoletos and Calle Serrano, decorated with pink tablecloths, fresh flowers, and paintings of country scenes. Chef Eduardo prepares French-Basque cuisine, with specialties including various crepes, *carré* (a prime cutlet or chop) of lamb, fresh sea bass, turbot, and hake, plus rich game dishes in season. Alfonso Castro, the knowledgeable sommelier, offers good wines and brandies. Dinner reservations are wise; at lunchtime, there's food at the bar. *Recoletos 7, tel. 91/431–4134. AE, DC, MC, V. Closed Sun. and Aug.*

$$$ EL CENADOR DEL PRADO. The name means "The Prado Dining
★ Room," and the settings are a Baroque salon and a plant-filled conservatory. The Cenador's innovative menu has French and Asian touches, as well as exotic Spanish dishes that rarely appear in restaurants. The house specialty is *patatas a la importancia* (sliced potatoes fried in a sauce of garlic, parsley, and clams); other possibilities include shellfish consommé with ginger ravioli, veal and eggplant in béchamel, and venison with prunes. For dessert try the *bartolillos* (custard-filled pastries). *C. del Prado 4, tel. 91/ 429–1561. AE, DC, MC, V. Closed Sun. and 1 wk in Aug. No lunch Sat.*

$$$ EL PESCADOR. Locals swear that seafood served in Madrid is
★ fresher than in the coastal towns where it was caught. That's probably an exaggeration, but El Pescador, one of Madrid's most respected seafood restaurants, makes it seem plausible. Stop for a drink at the bar and savor the aromas wafting from the kitchen, where skilled chefs dressed in fishermen's smocks

madrid dining

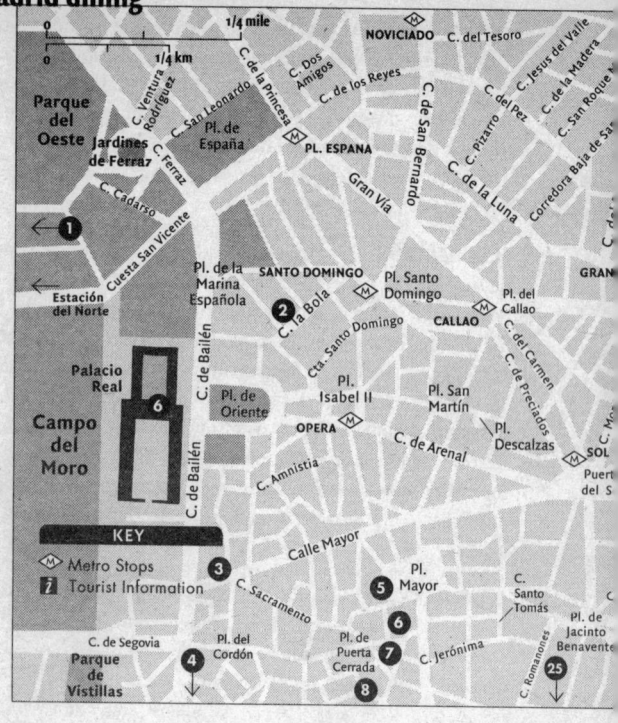

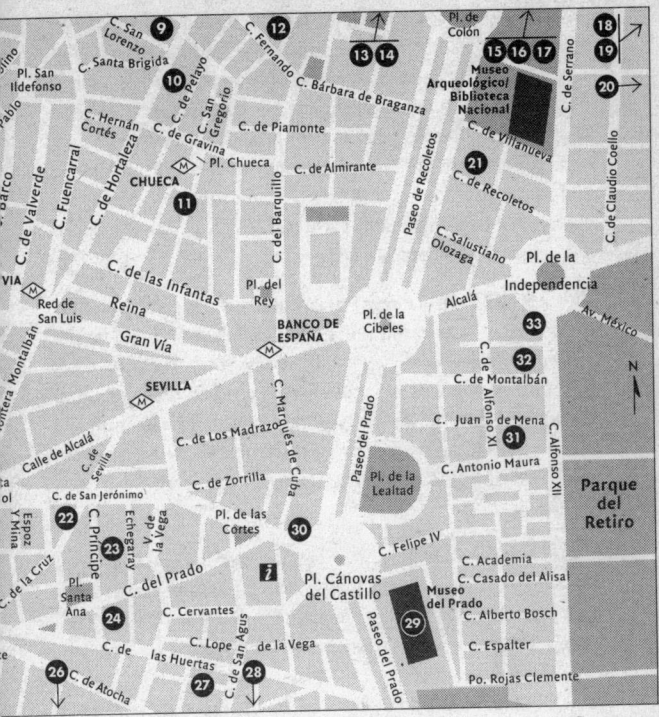

prepare shellfish just behind the counter. Among the tapas, the *salpicón de mariscos* (mussels, lobster, shrimp, and onions in vinaigrette) is incredible. The best dish on the dinner menu is *lenguado Evaristo* (grilled sole), named for the restaurant's owner. When it's busy, the place can be cheerful and noisy, with dockside-rustic decor: lobster-pot lamps, red-and-white-check tablecloths, and rough-hewn posts and beams. Unfortunately, the aging waiters can be disagreeably surly. *José Ortega y Gasset 75, tel. 91/ 402–1290. MC, V. Closed Sun. and Aug.*

$$$ GINZA SUSHI BAR. Madrid's first Japanese sushi bar is conveniently set opposite American Express and the Palace Hotel, near the Thyssen and Prado museums. The conveyor belt does a brisk business, with plates priced between 300 and 900 ptas., and there's a sit-down restaurant upstairs. The staff is cheerful, and Spain's fresh fish is perfect for the tasty morsels. You can reserve seats at the bar. *Plaza de las Cortes 3, tel. 91/429–7619. AE, DC, MC, V. Closed Mon.*

$$$ JULIÁN DE TOLOSA. This rustic yet designer-decorated spot on the corner of Cava Baja and Almendro is famous for *alubias pintas* (red kidney beans) from the Basque town of Tolosa. The *jabugo* ham and the two-person *txuletón* (28-oz. beefsteak) are excellent. Try a Basque *txakolí* (tart, young white wine) with your first course and a split of Ribera de Duero with the heavier end of the meal. Reservations are advised. *Cava Baja 18, tel. 91/365–8210. AE, DC, MC, V. Closed Sun.*

$$$ LA CAVA REAL. Wine connoisseurs love the intimate atmosphere of this small bar-restaurant, which was Madrid's first true wine bar when it opened in 1983. Still part of Spain's largest wine club (Warning: no beer!), it's also open to the public, smartly decorated in plush reds and dark browns. There are a staggering 350 wines on offer, including 50 by the glass. The charming and experienced maître d', Chema Gómez, can help you choose. Chef Javier Collar designs good-value menus around various wines, and the à la carte selection is plentiful, mainly *nueva cocina* with game in season as well as fancy desserts and cheeses. *Espronceda 34, tel. 91/442–5432. Reservations essential. AE, DC, MC, V. Closed Sun. and Aug.*

$$–$$$ **CASA PACO.** ★ This popular Castilian tavern wouldn't have looked out of place two or three centuries ago. Squeeze past the old, zinc-top bar, always crowded with Madrileños downing shots of Valdepeñas red wine, and into the tile dining rooms. People come here to feast on thick slabs of red meat, served sizzling on plates so hot that the meat continues to cook at your table. The beef is superb, and the Spanish consider overcooking a sin, so be prepared for looks of dismay if you ask for your meat well done (*bien hecho*). You order by weight, so remember that a *medio kilo* is more than a pound. To start, try the *pisto manchego* (the La Mancha version of ratatouille) or the classic Castilian *sopa de ajo* (garlic soup). *Puerta Cerrada 11, tel. 91/366–3166. Reservations essential. AE, DC, MC, V. Closed Sun. and Aug.*

$$–$$$ **IROCO.** This large, stylish, green-wall establishment is popular with businesspeople at the lunch hour and trendy folk in the evening. In summer, reservations are essential for tables on the garden patio, where Crown Prince Felipe has been spotted. The *nueva cocina* (nouvelle cuisine) is well presented, and the set lunch menu is good value. Classic dishes include prawn rolls, hake in green asparagus sauce, and chocolate mousse. *Velázquez 18, tel. 91/431–7381. Reservations essential. AE, DC, MC, V.*

$$–$$$ **LA GAMELLA.** ★ American-born chef Dick Stephens has created a new, reasonably priced menu at this perennially popular dinner spot. The sophisticated rust-red dining room, batik tablecloths, oversize plates, and attentive service remain the same, but much of the nouvelle cuisine has been replaced by more traditional fare, such as chicken in garlic, beef bourguignon, and steak tartare à la Jack Daniels. A few of the old signature dishes, like sausage-and-red-pepper quiche and bittersweet chocolate pâté, remain. The lunchtime *menú del día* is a great value. *Alfonso XII 4, tel. 91/532–4509. AE, DC, MC, V. Closed Sun. and Aug. 15–30. No lunch Sat.*

$$–$$$ **LAS CUEVAS DE LUIS CANDELAS.** Hidden just off the southwest corner of the Plaza Mayor, this "cave" is said to be the oldest tavern in Madrid and feels like the medieval cellar of a Spanish mansion. Popular with locals as well as travelers, the tavern is divided into three sections. You're greeted by a host dressed as the 19th-century bandit himself, and you enter through a long bar where noisy regulars drink and munch tapas. A low stone archway leads to a quieter area where you can sit on low benches, drink from a ceramic jar, and eat *raciones* of such tapas as mushrooms in garlic and cured ham. Farther inside the "cave" are the dining areas, with painted scenes of old Madrid. Barbecued meats are the specialty, and portions are huge and heavy—for a light dinner, stay in the tapas lounge. A guitar player strolls between the ancient rooms, adding to the enchanting, if slightly touristy, atmosphere. *Cuchilleros 1, tel. 91/366–5428. AE, MC, V.*

$$ **BOTÍN.** The *Guinness Book of Records* calls this the world's oldest
★ restaurant (1725), and Hemingway called it the best. The latter claim may be a bit over the top, but the restaurant is excellent and extremely charming (and so successful that the owners opened a "branch" in Miami, Florida). There are four floors of tile, wood-beam dining rooms, and if you're seated upstairs you'll pass ovens dating back centuries. Musical groups called *tunas* often drop in to meander among the hordes in traditional garb. Specialties are *cochinillo asado* (roast suckling pig) and *cordero asado* (roast lamb), but you might also try the *estofada de perdiz* (stewed partridge). It is said that Goya washed dishes here before he made it as a painter. *Cuchilleros 17, off Plaza Mayor, tel. 91/366–4217. AE, DC, MC, V.*

$$ **CASA CIRIACO.** One of Madrid's most traditional restaurants, Ciriaco has hosted a long list of Spain's illustrious, from royalty to philosophers, painters, and bullfighters. Typical of what Madrid does best, simple home cooking in an unpretentious environment, Casa Ciriaco will serve you a flagon of Valdepeñas or a split of a Rioja reserva to accompany the specialty of *perdiz con favas* (partridge with broadbeans). The *judias con liebre* (white beans with hare) is another favorite. *Calle Mayor 84, tel. 91/559–5066. AE, MC, V. Closed Wed. and Aug.*

$$ CASA LASTRA. Established in 1926, this little Asturian restaurant-bar is popular with locals in the charming Lavapié district. It has a rustic feel, its half-tile walls strung with relics from the Asturian countryside, including wooden clogs and cow bells along with sausages and garlic. Specialties include *fabada* (Asturian ham and white-bean stew), *fabas con almejas* (white beans with clams), and *queso de cabrales*, Spain's super-tangy blue cheese, made in the Picos de Europa from a mixture of milk from cows, goats, and sheep. Desserts include baked apples. Great hunks of crisp bread and hard Asturian cider can complement a hearty meal on a 2,200-pta. weekday set menu. *Olivar 3, tel. 91/369–0837. AE, MC, V. Closed Wed. and July. No dinner Sun.*

$$ CASA VALLEJO. With its homey dining room, friendly staff, creative menu, and reasonable prices, Casa Vallejo is a well-kept secret of low-budget foodies. Try the tomato, zucchini, and cheese tart or artichokes and clams to start; follow up with duck in prune sauce or meatballs made with lamb, almonds, and pine nuts. The fudge-and-raspberry pie alone is worth the trip. *San Lorenzo 9, tel. 91/308–6158. Reservations essential. MC, V. Closed Aug. and Sun. No dinner Mon.*

$$ LA BOLA. First opened as a *botellería* (wine shop) in 1802, La Bola ★ developed slowly into a tapas bar and eventually into a full-fledged restaurant. Tradition is the main draw; blood-red paneling outside beckons you into the original bar and the cozy dining nooks, decorated with polished wood, Spanish tile, and lace curtains. The restaurant still belongs to the founding family, with the seventh generation currently in training. Dinner is served, but the house specialty is that quintessential Madrid meal *cocido a la madrileña*, served only at lunch and accompanied by crusty bread and a hearty red wine. *C. de la Bola 5, tel. 91/547–6930. No credit cards. No dinner Sun.*

$$ LA CACHARRERÍA. The name of this restaurant means "junkyard," and it's reflected in the decor—a mix of dusty calico, old lace, and gilt mirrors, all tucked into the medieval quarter. The cooking, however, is upscale, with a market-based menu that changes daily and an excellent selection of wines. Venison stew and tuna steaks with *cava* (sparkling white wine from Catalonia) and leeks have been among the specialties. Save room for the homemade lemon tart. *Moreria 9, tel. 91/365-3930. AE, DC, MC, V. Closed Sun.*

$-$$ TABERNA CARMENCITA. A classic little spot just two minutes' north of the Gran Vía—Calle Alcalá intersection is an old Madrid favorite for lunches and light dinners. Now part of priest-restaurateur Patxo de Lezama's sprawling gastronomic empire (which extends to Washington, DC), this ceramic-tile tavern has managed to retain much of the atmosphere it had in the mid-20th century, when Carmencita herself cared for customers as though they were long-lost children. The *chipirones en su tinta* (squid in its ink) and *sopa de pescado* (fish soup) are reliably tasty. *Libertad 16, tel. 91/531-6612. AE, MC, V. Closed Sat. lunch and Sun.*

$ CASA MINGO. Resembling an Asturian cider tavern, Casa Mingo
★ is built into a stone wall beneath the Estación del Norte, across the street from the hermitage of San Antonio de la Florida. It's a bustling place; you share long plank tables with other diners, and the only items on the menu are succulent roast chicken, salad, and sausages, all to be taken with *sidra* (hard cider). Small tables are set up on the sidewalk in summer. If you don't come early (1 for lunch, 8:30 for dinner), you may have to wait for a table. *Paseo de la Florida 2, tel. 91/547-7918. Reservations not accepted. No credit cards.*

$ CHAMPAGNERÍA GALA. Hidden on a back street not far from Calle Atocha and the Reina Sofía museum, this cheerful Mediterranean restaurant is usually packed thanks to its fixed-price three-course menus with wine, which offer a choice of paellas, *fideuas* (paellas with noodles instead of rice), risottos, and hearty bean stews. Only *cava*, Catalan sparkling wine, costs extra. The front dining area is

When you pack your MCI Calling Card, it's like packing your loved ones along too.

Your MCI Calling Card is the easy way to stay in touch when you travel. Use it to call to and from over 125 countries. Plus, every time you call, you can earn frequent flier miles. So wherever your travels take you, call home with your MCI Calling Card. It's even easy to get one. Just visit **www.mci.com/worldphone**.

EASY TO CALL WORLDWIDE

1. Just enter the WorldPhone® access number of the country you're calling from.
2. Enter or give the operator your MCI Calling Card number.
3. Enter or give the number you're calling.

Australia ◆	1-800-881-100	Ireland	1-800-55-1001
China	108-12	Italy ◆	172-1022
France ◆	0-800-99-0019	Japan ◆	00539-121▶
Germany	0800-888-8000	South Africa	0800-99-0011
Hong Kong	800-96-1121	Spain	900-99-0014
		United Kingdom	0800-89-0222

◆ Public phones may require deposit of coin or phone card for dial tone. ▶ Regulation does not permit intra-Japan calls.

EARN FREQUENT FLIER MILES

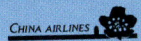

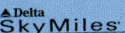

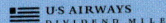

Money From Home In Minutes.

If you're stuck for cash on your travels, don't panic. Millions of people trust Western Union to transfer money in minutes to over 185 countries and over 95,000 locations worldwide. Our record of safety and reliability is second to none. You can even send money by phone without leaving home by using a credit card. For more information, call Western Union: USA 1-800-325-6000, Canada 1-800-235-0000.

www.westernunion.com

WESTERN UNION | MONEY TRANSFER

The fastest way to send money worldwide.

a kaleidoscope of painted color, particularly red; the back area incorporates trees and plants in a glassed-in patio. *Moratín 22, tel. 91/429–2562. Reservations essential. No credit cards.*

$ CIAO. Always noisy and packed with happy diners, Ciao is Madrid's best Italian restaurant. Homemade pastas, like tagliatelle with wild mushrooms and *panzarotti* stuffed with spinach and ricotta, are popular as inexpensive main courses; but the kitchen also turns out credible versions of osso buco and veal scallopini, accompanied by a good selection of Italian wines. The decor—mirrored walls and sleek black furniture—convincingly evokes fashionable Milan. A second location (Apodaca 20, tel. 91/447–0036), run by the owner's sons and daughter, also serves pizza. *Argensola 7, tel. 91/ 308–2519. Reservations essential. AE, DC, MC, V. Closed Sept., Sun., No lunch Sat.*

$ LA BIOTIKA. A vegetarian's dream in the heart of the bar district just east of Plaza Santa Ana, this small, cozy restaurant serves macrobiotic vegetarian cuisine seven days a week. Enormous salads, hearty soups, fresh bread, and creative tofu dishes make the meal flavorful as well as healthy. A small shop at the entrance sells macrobiotic groceries. *Amor de Dios 3, tel. 91/429–0780. No credit cards.*

$ LA TRUCHA. ★ At either of its two locations, this Andalusian deep-fry specialist is one of the happiest places in Madrid. The staff is perennially jovial, and the house specialty, *trucha la truchana* (crisped trout stuffed with ample garlic and diced *jabugo* ham) is a work of art worthy of inclusion in one of the nearby museums. Other star entrées are *chopitos* (baby squid), *pollo al ajillo* (chunks of chicken in crisped garlic), and *espárragos trigueros* (wild asparagus). *Jarras* (pitchers) of chilled Valdepeñas, a young Beaujolais-like claret, seem to function as laughing gas in this magic little bistro. The Nuñez de Arce store, just down from the Hotel Reina Victoria, is usually less crowded. *Manuel Fernandez y Gonzalez 3; Nuñez de Arce 6, tel. 91/429–3778. AE, MC, V. Closed Sun. Nuñez de Arce branch also closed Aug.*

Eating Well is the Best Revenge

Eating out is a major part of every travel experience. It's a chance to explore flavors you don't find at home. And often the walking you do on vacation means that you can dig in without guilt.

START AT THE TOP By all means take in a really good restaurant or two while you're on the road. A trip is a time to kick back and savor the pleasures of the palate. Read up on the culinary scene before you leave home. Check out representative menus on the Web—some chefs have gone electronic. And ask friends who have just come back. Then reserve a table as far in advance as you can, remembering that the best establishments book up months in advance. Remember that some good restaurants require you to reconfirm the day before or the day of your meal. Then again, some really good places will call you, so make sure to leave a number where you can be reached.

ADVENTURES IN EATING A trip is the perfect opportunity to try food you can't get at home. So leave yourself open to try an ethnic food that's not represented where you live or to eat fruits and vegetables you've never heard of. One of them may become your next favorite food.

BEYOND GUIDEBOOKS You can rely on the restaurants you find in these pages. But also look for restaurants on your own. When you're ready for lunch, ask people you meet where they eat. Look for tiny holes-in-the-wall with a loyal following and the best burgers or crispiest pizza crust. Find out about local chains whose fame rests upon a single memorable dish. There's hardly a food-lover who doesn't relish the chance to share a favorite place. It's fun to come up with your own special find—and asking about food is a great way to start a conversation.

SAMPLE LOCAL FLAVORS Do check out the specialties. Is there a special brand of ice cream or a special dish that you simply must try?

HAVE A PICNIC Every so often eat al fresco. Grocery shopping gives you a whole different view of a place.

$ NABUCCO. With pastel-washed walls and subtle lighting from gigantic, wrought-iron candelabras, this pizzeria and trattoria is a trendy but elegant haven in gritty Chueca. Fresh bread sticks and garlic olive oil show up within minutes of your arrival. The spinach, ricotta, and walnut ravioli is heavenly, and this may be the only Italian restaurant in Madrid where you can order (California-style?) barbecue-chicken pizza, although the four-cheese one is good as well. Considering the ambience and quality, the bill is a pleasant surprise. *Hortaleza 108, tel. 91/310–0611. AE, MC, V.*

In This Chapter

Updated by George Semler

shopping

MADRID HAS FAR MORE TO OFFER than Lladró porcelain and bullfighting posters—Spain has become one of the world's centers for design of every kind. You'll have no trouble finding traditional crafts, such as ceramics, guitars, and leather goods (albeit not at countryside prices), but at this point the city is more like Rodeo Drive than the bargain bin. Known for contemporary furniture and decorative items as well as chic clothing, shoes, and jewelry, Spain's capital has become stiff competition for Barcelona. Most shops accept most major credit cards.

DEPARTMENT STORES

EL CORTE INGLÉS. Spain's largest department store carries the best selection of everything, from auto parts to groceries to designer fashions. *Tel. 901/122122 for general information; 902/400222 for ticket sales. Preciados 3, tel. 91/531–9619; Goya 76 and 87, tel. 91/432–9300; Princesa 56, tel. 91/454–6000; Serrano 47, tel. 91/432–5490; Raimundo Fernández Villaverde 79, tel. 91/418–8800.*

ZARA. For those with young tastes and slim pocketbooks (picture hip clothes that you'll throw away in about six months), Zara has the latest looks for men, women, and children. *Centro Comercial ABC, Serrano 61, tel. 91/575–6334; Gran Vía 32, tel. 91/522–9727; Princesa 63, tel. 91/543–2415; Conde de Peñalver 4, tel. 91/435–4135.*

SHOPPING DISTRICTS

Madrid has two main shopping areas. The first is in the center of town, around the **PUERTA DEL SOL,** and includes the major department stores (El Corte Inglés, the French music-and-book chain FNAC, etc.) and a large number of mid-range shops in the streets nearby. The second area, far more elegant and expensive, is in the northwestern **SALAMANCA** district, bounded roughly by Serrano, Goya, and Conde de Peñalver. These streets, just off the Plaza de Colón (particularly Calle Serrano), have the widest selection of smart boutiques and designer fashions—think Prada, Armani, and Donna Karan New York, as well as renowned Spanish designers such as Sybilla and Josep Font-Luz Diaz. If you're in the market for clothes, you may find that Spaniards, like Italians, favor brown tones; cool palettes don't prevail, though of course black is readily available.

GALERÍAS DEL PRADO (Plaza de las Cortes 7) is an attractive mall tucked under the Palace Hotel on the Paseo del Prado. Shop here for fine books, gourmet foods, clothing, leather goods, art, and more. Madrid's newest mall is a four-decker: the **CENTRO COMERCIAL ABC** (Paseo de la Castellana 34/Serrano 61), named for the daily newspaper founded on the premises in the 19th century. The building is a beautifully restored landmark with an ornate tile facade; inside, a large café is surrounded by shops of all kinds, including leather stores and hairdressers. The fourth-floor restaurant has a rooftop terrace with scenic urban views. For street-chic shopping closer to medieval Madrid, check out the playful window displays at the **MADRID FUSION CENTRO DE MODA** (Plaza Tirso de Molina 15, tel. 91/369–0018), where up-and-coming Spanish design houses fill five floors with faux furs, funky jewelry, and Madrid's most eccentric collection of shoes.

FLEA MARKET

On Sunday morning, Calle de Ribera de Curtidores is closed to traffic and jammed with outdoor booths selling everything under the sun—its weekly transformation into **EL RASTRO**. The crowds grow so thick that it takes a while just to advance a few feet amid the hawkers and the gawkers. A word of warning: pickpockets abound here. Hang on to your purse and wallet, and be especially careful if you choose to bring a camera. The flea market sprawls into most of the surrounding streets, with certain areas specializing in particular products. Many of the goods sold here are wildly overpriced.

But what goods! The Rastro has everything from antique furniture to exotic parrots and cuddly puppies; from pirated cassette tapes of flamenco music to key chains emblazoned with symbols of the CNT, Spain's old anarchist trade union. Practice your Spanish by bargaining with the vendors over paintings, colorful Gypsy oxen yokes, heraldic iron gates, new and used clothes, and even hashish pipes. They may not lower their prices, but sometimes they'll throw in a handmade bracelet or a stack of postcards to sweeten the deal.

Off the Ribera are two *galerías*, courtyards where small shops offer higher-quality, higher-price antiques and other goods. Near the top of the Rastro, stop into **BAR SANTURCE** (C. Amazonas 14) for sardines, Galician *pimientos de Padrón* (red peppers, some hot), and calamari. Plaza General Vara del Rey has some of the Rastro's best antiques, and the streets beyond—Calles Mira el Río Alta and Mira el Río Baja—have some truly magnificent junk and bric-a-brac. The whole spectacle shuts down shortly after 2 PM, just in time for a street party to start in the area known as La Latina, centered on the bar El Viajero in Plaza Humilladero.

SPECIALTY STORES
Books

CASA DEL LIBRO (Maestro Victoria 3, tel. 91/521–4898), not far from the Puerta del Sol, has an impressive collection of English-language books, including detailed city guides and translated Spanish classics. It's also a good source for maps, cookbooks, and gifts. **BOOKSELLERS** (José Abascal 48, tel. 91/442–8104), just off the upper Castellana near the Hotel Miguel Angel, has a large selection of books in English. For travel books, including books about Madrid in English, seek out **TIERRA DE FUEGO** (C. del Pez 21, tel. 91/521–3962) in the Barrio de Maravillas, two blocks north of the central Gran Vía.

Established in 1950, **LA TIENDA VERDE** (Maudes 23 and 38, tel. 91/535–3810) is a paradise for outdoor enthusiasts planning hikes, mountain-climbing expeditions, spelunking trips, and so forth, with detailed maps and Spanish-language guidebooks.

Boutiques and Fashion

ADOLFO DOMÍNGUEZ (Serrano 96, tel. 91/576–7053; and six other locations) is one of Spain's best-known designers, with lines for both men and women. Prominent young designer **JESÚS DEL POZO** (Almirante 9, tel. 91/531–3646) also caters to both sexes; his boutique is an excellent, if pricey, place to try on some classic Spanish style. Since the turn of the 20th century **SESEÑA** (De la Cruz 23, tel. 91/531–6840) has outfitted international celebrities in wool and velvet capes, some lined with red satin. **SYBILLA** (Jorge Juan 12, tel. 91/578–1322) is the studio of Spain's best-known female designer, whose fluid dresses and hand-knit sweaters in natural colors and fabrics have made her a favorite with Danish supermodel Helena Christensen.

Ceramics

ANTIGUA CASA TALAVERA (Isabel la Católica 2, tel. 91/547–3417) is the best of Madrid's numerous ceramics shops. Despite the name, the finest ware sold here is from Manises, near Valencia, but the blue-and-yellow Talavera ceramics are also excellent. **CÁNTARO** (Flor Baja 8, tel. 91/547–9514) sells excellent handmade ceramics. **CERÁMICA EL ALFAR** (Claudio Coello 112, tel. 91/411–3587) is laden with pottery from all corners of Spain. **SAGARDELOS** (Zurbano 46, tel. 91/310–4830), specializing in modern Spanish ceramics from Galicia, has excellent selections of breakfast sets, coffee pots, and objets d'art.

Crafts and Design

CASA JULIA (Almirante 1, tel. 91/522–0270) is an artistic showcase, with two floors of tasteful antiques, paintings by up-and-coming artists, and furniture in experimental designs. It's a great place to hunt for nontraditional souvenirs. **EL ARCO** (Plaza Mayor 9, tel. 91/365–2680) has a good selection of contemporary handicrafts from all over Spain, including modern ceramics, handblown glassware, jewelry, and leather items as well as a whimsical collection of pendulum clocks.

Fans

CASA DE DIEGO (Puerta del Sol 12, tel. 91/522–6643), established in 1853, stocks a classic collection of fans, umbrellas, and classic Spanish walking sticks with ornamented silver handles. The British royal family buys autograph fans here—white kid-skin fans for signing on special occasions.

Food and Wine

The Club Gourmet sections in stores present a wide choice of Spanish wines, olive oils, and foodstuffs. Handily located near Plaza Santa Ana and Plaza de les Cortés, **GONZÁLEZ** (Calle Léon 21, tel. 91/429–5618) features fine Spanish wines, olive oils, cheeses, hams, dried pulses, and other foods. Sample the offerings at the wine bar at back. **LAVININA** (José Ortega y Gasset 16, tel. 91/426–0604) claims to be the largest wine store in Europe, and does have a massive selection of bottles, books, and bar accessories. The upscale chain **MALLORCA** (Velázquez 59, tel. 91/431–9909; Serrano 6, tel. 91/577–1859; Centro Comercial, Goya 6, tel. 91/577–2123) sells prepared meals, cocktail canapés, chocolates, and wines, and has tapas counters for sampling. Just across from eating holes Los Gabrieles and La Trucha, behind Plaza Santa Ana, **MARIANO AGUADO** (C. Echegaray 19, tel. 91/429–6088) is a charming 150-year-old wine store with a quaint ceiling mural and a wide selection of fine wines and spirits.

Hats

Founded in 1894, **CASA YUSTAS** (Plaza Mayor 30, tel. 91/366–5084) carries an amazing assortment of headgear, from the old three-corner, patent-leather hats of the Guardia Civil to fashionable ladies' hats to Basque berets to black Andalusian *sombreros de mayoral*. Designed as hands-free umbrellas for the rainy Cantabrian coast, Basque berets are much wider than those worn by the French, and make excellent gifts.

Kitchenware

A pleasing mixture of tradition and high style, **ALAMBIQUE** (C. de la Bola, tel. 91/547–8827), on Plaza de la Encarnación, has everything from earthenware and Asturian cider glasses to cookbooks and a cooking school.

Leather Goods

On a street full of bargain shoe stores (*muestrarios*), **CALIGAE** (Augusto Figueroa 27, tel. 91/531–5343) is probably the best of the bunch. Posh **LOEWE** (Serrano 26 and 34, tel. 91/577–6056; Gran Vía 8, tel. 91/532–7024; Palace Hotel, tel. 91/429–8530) features ultra–high quality designer purses, accessories, and clothing made of buttery-soft leather in dyed, jewel-like colors. Prices can hit the stratosphere. **TENORIO** (Plaza de la Provincia 6, tel. 91/366–4440) is where you'll find those fine old boots of Spanish leather, made to order with workmanship that should last a lifetime and is priced accordingly, starting at 110,000 ptas.

Music

JOSÉ RAMIREZ (C. La Paz 8, tel. 91/531–4229) has provided Spain and the rest of the world with guitars since 1882, and his store includes a museum of antique instruments. Prices for new ones start at 15,000 ptas., though the top concert models are closer to 1,000,000 ptas. **REAL MÚSICA** (Carlos III 1, tel. 91/541–3007), around the corner from the Teatro Real, is a music lover's dream, with books, CDs, sheet music, memorabilia, guitars, and other instruments, and a knowledgeable staff.

In This Chapter

Updated by George Semler

outdoor activities and sports

MADRILEÑOS ARE A VIGOROUS, joyful lot, famous for their ability to defy sleep. They embrace their city's vibrant sports activities with as much zest as they do its cultural opportunities and nightlife. And you need only witness a bullfight at Las Ventas or a Real Madrid soccer match at Santiago Bernabeu Stadium to see that, in some cases, culture and sport are one in the same. What's more, Spain's fair weather is ideally suited to spending time outdoors virtually year-round. In summer, however, it's best to restrict physical activity to early morning or late afternoon.

PARTICIPANT SPORTS

Golf

GOLF OLIVAR DE LA HINOJOSA (Avda. Dublín s/n, tel. 91/721–1889), in Campo de las Naciones outside town, is open to the public with two courses (one 18 holes, one 9) and golf lessons.

Jogging

Your best bet is the **PARQUE DEL RETIRO,** where one path circles the entire park and numerous others weave their way under trees and through formal gardens. The **CASA DE CAMPO** is crisscrossed by numerous, sunnier trails.

Swimming

Madrid has the perfect antidote to the dry, sometimes intense heat of the summer months—a superb system of clean, popular, well-run municipal swimming pools (admission about 350 ptas.). The biggest and best—fitted with a comfortable, tree-shaded restaurant—is in the **CASA DE CAMPO** (take the metro to Lago and walk up the hill a few yards; tel. 91/463–0050). Another good choice in the city center is the **PISCINA CANAL ISABEL II** (Plaza Juan Zorrila, entrance off Avda. de Filipinas, no phone), with diving boards and a wading pool for kids.

Tennis

CLUB DE TENIS CHAMARTÍN (Federico Salmon 2, tel. 91/345–2500) is open to the public with 28 courts. There are also public courts in the **CASA DE CAMPO** and on the Avenida de Vírgen del Puerto, behind the Palacio Real; the tourist office has details.

SPECTATOR SPORTS
Bullfighting

Bullfighting is really a spectacle, not a sport. For those not turned off by the death of six bulls every Sunday afternoon from April to early November, it offers all the excitement of a major stadium event. Nowhere in the world is bullfighting better than at Madrid's **LAS VENTAS** (C. Alcalá 231, tel. 91/356–2200; metro: Las Ventas), formally called the Plaza de Toros Monumental. The sophisticated audience follows taurine matters closely, and the uninitiated might be baffled by their reactions: cheers and hoots can be hard to distinguish, and it can take years to understand what prompts the wrath of such a hard-to-please crowd. For a traveler, this can be the most entertaining part of the experience. Tickets can be purchased at the ring or, for a 20% surcharge, at one of the agencies on Calle Victoria, just off the Puerta del Sol. Most *corridas* start in late afternoon, and the best fights of all—the world's top displays of bullfighting—come during the three weeks of consecutive daily events that mark the feast of San Isidro, in May. Tickets can be tough to get through normal channels, but they're always available from scalpers in the Calle Victoria and at the stadium. You can bargain, but even Spaniards pay prices of perhaps 10 times the face value—up to 20,000 ptas. or even more.

NEED A BREAK? **LA PUERTA GRANDE** (Pedro Heredia 23, tel. 91/355–1087) is an atmospheric bullfight bar–restaurant near the bullring. Have a tapa or a full meal, perhaps with *rabo de toro* (bull's-tail stew) if mad-cow disease doesn't do away with this dish. Enthusiastic owners José and Miguel Martín have entertained *aficionados* since 1991; to find the place, cross Alcalá in front of the ring, walk up and turn left down Maestro Alonso.

Soccer

Spain's number-one sport is known locally as *fútbol*. Madrid has three major teams, Real Madrid, Atlético Madrid, and Rayo Vallecano. The enormous **ESTADIO SANTIAGO BERNABEU** (Paseo de la Castellana 140, tel. 91/398–4300), which seats 75,000, is home to Real Madrid, winner of the 2000 European Champion's Cup. Atlético Madrid attempts its return into the first division at the **ESTADIO VICENTE CALDERÓN** (Virgen del Puerto 67, tel. 91/366–4704 or 91/364–0888), on the outskirts of town. First-division surprise Rayo Vallecano plays at **ESTADIO DEL RAYO** (Arroyo del Olivar 49, tel. 91/478–2253). You generally have to stand in line at the stadium to get tickets, but some are available at Corte Inglés department stores.

In This Chapter

Updated by *George Semler*

nightlife and the arts

NIGHTLIFE—OR LA MARCHA, as the Spanish fondly call it—reaches legendary heights in Spain's capital. It has been said that Madrileños rarely sleep, largely because they spend so much time in bars—not drunk, but socializing in the easy, sophisticated way that's unique to this city. This is true of old as well as young, and it's not uncommon for children to play on the sidewalks past midnight while multigenerational families and friends convene over coffee or cocktails at an outdoor café. The streets best known for their social scenes, however, do tend to attract a younger clientele; these include Huertas, Moratín, Segovia, Victoria, and the areas around the Plaza Santa Ana and the Plaza de Anton Martín. The adventurous may want to explore the scruffier bar district around the Plaza Dos de Mayo, in the Malasaña area, where trendy, smoke-filled hangouts line both sides of Calle San Vicente Ferrer. A few blocks east are the haunts of Chueca, where tattoo studios and street-chic boutiques break up the endless alleys of gay and lesbian bars, techno discos, and after-hours clubs.

BARS AND TAVERNS

The practice of spending the evening wandering from bar to bar and eating tapas is so popular that the Spanish have a verb to describe it: *tapear*. Madrid's selection is endless; the best-known tapas bars are the *cuevas* clustered around Cava de San Miguel.

Bars

ALHAMBRA. This one-room tavern has been serving excellent wine, beer, and tapas to a gregarious crowd since 1929. Alhambra opens at an eye-popping 9:30 AM; around midnight it fills up, the windows get steamy, and the crowd does pseudo-*sevillana* dance moves to traditional music. When it's packed, they jump right onto the wooden tabletops without missing a beat. *Victoria 9, tel. 91/521–0708.*

CAFÉ GIJÓN. Madrid's most famous literary café has hosted high-brow *tertulias*, discussion groups that meet regularly to hash out the political and artistic issues of the day, since the 19th century. *Paseo de Recoletos 21, tel. 91/521–5425.*

EL CLANDESTINO. Run by a French couple who seem to be Spaniards at heart, this bar-café is a hidden, low-key hot spot with a local following: atmosphere without attitude. Impromptu jam sessions are rounded out by two floors alternating mellow jazz with house and ambient music. *Barquillo 34, tel. 91/521–5563.*

HARD ROCK CAFE. Wildly popular with young Spaniards, Madrid's version of the U.S. classic opened in 1994, serving up the usual drinks, burgers, and salads with a heavy dose of loud music. *Paseo de la Castellana 2, tel. 91/436–4340.*

LOS GABRIELES. This building is featured in most Madrid tourist literature for its remarkable tiled walls—advertisements from the turn of the 20th century, when this was a high-class brothel. Drinks are unusually pricey. *Echegaray 17, tel. 91/429–6261.*

OLIVER. Here are two bars in one: afternoons and evenings, an upstairs lounge and restaurant; late at night, a full-fledged Chueca disco in the brick-lined basement cavern. *Almirante 12, tel. 91/521–7379.*

PALACIO DE GAVIRIA. Hidden away on a tawdry commercial street between Puerta del Sol and the Royal Palace, this restored 19th-century palace was allegedly built to house one of Queen Isabel II's lovers. An exotic maze, it now offers drinks in a sophisticated setting, with a disco and frequent late-night jazz in the mirrored ballroom. *Arenal 9, tel. 91/526–6069.*

SOHO. Something of a slice of New York in the Salamanca district, Soho has an eclectic menu that includes exotic island drinks as well as Spanish variants of Tex-Mex cuisine. It's filled with rap and reggae fans. *Jorge Juan 50, tel. 91/577-8973. Closed Sun.*

TABERNA DE ANTONIO SANCHEZ. Thought to be the oldest tavern in Madrid, this historic spot was traced by the late critic and *literato* Antonio Diaz-Cañabate to the late 18th century. Order wine and tapas at the old zinc bar in front; head to the back for a full meal. *Mesón de Paredes 13, tel. 91/539-7826.*

VIVA MADRID. This extremely popular bar has a Brassai motif and a serious personality. Packed with both Spaniards and foreigners, it has become something of a singles scene. There are tables and a small selection of bar food in the rear. *Manuel Fernández y González 7, tel. 91/429-3640.*

Tapas Bars

A *tapa* is a bit of food that often comes free with a drink; it might be a few olives, a mussel in vinaigrette, a sardine, or spicy potatoes. You can also order a larger plate of this kind of snack, called a *ración*, meant to be shared. The best place to start a tapa tour is near the Plaza Santa Ana or in the *mésones* built into the wall beneath the Plaza Mayor, along Cava de San Miguel. Each bar here specializes in a different tapa—for example, potato-and-egg tortillas (a Spanish tortilla is an omelet of sorts, not to be confused with the Mexican tortilla), garlicky mushrooms, or a small wedge of *empanada de atún*, a pastry stuffed with tuna, egg, and onions.

BOCAÍTO. This cozy spot with three doors on Calle Libertad has twin bars and a restaurant serving no fewer than 130 specialties, all lovingly prepared. The *pescaito* (deep-fried whitebait) is the best in Madrid. *Libertad 6, tel. 91/532-1219.*

EL ABUELO. A legendary favorite even in the tapa-saturated Plaza Santa Ana area, El Abuelo (The Grandfather) serves only two tapas—and does them better than anyone else: grilled shrimp and shrimp sautéed with garlic. House tradition is to drink the sweet, red homemade house wine while tossing shrimp shells onto the floor. *Victoria 12, tel. 91/521–2319.*

EL REY DE PIMIENTO. This bar serves some 40 different kinds of tapas, including, in keeping with its name (The Pepper King), roasted red pimientos as well as the intermittently hot pimientos *de padrón. Plaza Puerta Cerrada 4, tel. 91/365–2473.*

EL VENTORRILLO. Try to come here between May and October, when tables are set up in the shady park of Las Vistillas overlooking the city's western edge. Specialties include croquettes and mushrooms. This is Madrid's best place to watch the sun go down. *C. Bailén 14, tel. 91/366–3578.*

GONZÁLEZ. Founded in 1931, González is run by Vicente Carmona, once a professor of Spanish literature in the United States. The smart, trendy deli in front sells (and will ship) the best Spanish wines, olive oils, liqueurs, hams, cheeses, cold cuts, and pastries. The paneled wine bar in back is a great place to sample the wares. *C. Léon 12, tel. 91/429–5618.*

LA CHATA. Locals frequent this stylized *castizo* tapas bar, its walls and tree-trunk beams festooned with hams, sausages, chili peppers, and bullfight photos. You get an excellent free tapa with a drink; then choose from an array of snacks on display or some great *revuelto con ajetes* (scrambled eggs with green garlic tops). A slate shows wines available by the glass. *Cava Baja 24, tel. 91/366–1458.*

LA DOLORES. Crowded and noisy, this wonderful bar is rightly reputed to serve the best draft beer in Madrid. Located just behind the Palace Hotel, it has very few tables in back. *Plaza de Jesús 4, tel. 91/429–2243.*

LA TRUCHA. Locals praise the exquisite tapas and the medieval-inn decor, hung with hams and garlic. House favorites are the enormous *plato de pescaditos fritos,* an assortment of fried fish, and *plato de ahumados*, an assortment of smoked-fish delicacies on toast. A terrace invites alfresco nibbling in summer. *Manuel Fernández y González 3, tel. 91/429–5833.*

MESÓN GALLEGO. This hole-in-the-wall that serves wonderfully hearty Galician potato soup (a famous cure for those who've drunk too much) called *caldo gallego*. Not for everyone is the *Ribeiro*, the somewhat acidic white wine made with grapes from Galician riverbanks. *León 4, tel. 91/429–8997.*

MUSEO DEL JAMÓN. A small Madrid chain of tapas bars, the Ham Museum has become an institution. Look for the window full of dangling hams with hoofs. The best tapas are, of course, the air-cured hams, which come from all over the country. Don't be daunted by the variety; go for ordinary *serrano* or, if you feel like a splurge, the delicious, acorn-fed *ibérico de bellota*. *Carrera de San Jerónimo 6, tel. 91/458–0163; Mayor 7, tel. 91/531–4550; Paseo del Prado 44, tel. 91/420–2414.*

TABERNA DE CIEN VINOS. Popular with wine buffs on Madrid's tapas circuit, this wine bar is tucked into a charming old house with wooden shutters and stone columns. You can order a wide selection of Spanish wines by the glass, and the *raciones* border on gourmet. *Nuncio 17, tel. 91/365–4704.*

Cabaret

BERLIN CABARET (Costanilla de San Pedro 11, tel. 91/366–2034) professes to provide authentic cabaret as it was performed in Berlin in the '30s. (These days the audience is quite different.) Combining magic, chorus girls, and ribald comedy, it draws an eccentric crowd for vintage café theater. On weekends, the absurd fun lasts until daybreak.

Discos

Madrid's oldest and hippest disco for wild, all-night dancing to an international music mix is **EL SOL** (C. Jardines 3, tel. 91/532–6490), open 'til 5:30 AM. There's live music around midnight

Thursday, Friday, and Saturday. **AVE NOX** (Lagasca 31, tel. 91/576–9715) is a torrid new music bar–disco in a converted chapel: vaulted ceiling, choir loft, and all. **JOY ESLAVA** (C. Arenal 11, tel. 91/366–3733), a downtown disco in a converted theater, is an old standby. **PACHÁ** (Barceló 11, tel. 91/447–0128), one of Spain's infamous chain discos, is always energetic. **FORTUNY** (Fortuny 34, tel. 91/319–0588) attracts a celebrity crowd, especially in summer, when the lush outdoor patio opens for partying under the stars. Put on your best dancing shoes: the door is ultraselective. Salsa has become a fixture in Madrid; check out the most spectacular moves at **AZÚCAR** (Sugar; Paseo Reina Cristina 7, tel. 91/501–6107).

Nightclubs

Jazz, rock, flamenco, and classical music are all popular in Madrid's many small clubs.

AMADIS. Here, telephones on every table encourage people to call each other with invitations to dance. *Covarrubias 42 (underneath Luchana Cinema), tel. 91/446–0036.*

CAFÉ CENTRAL. Madrid's best-known jazz venue is chic and well run, and the musicians are often internationally known. Performances are usually from 10 PM to midnight. *Plaza de Ángel 10, tel. 91/369–4143.*

CAFE DEL FORO. This funky, friendly club on the edge of Malasaña has live music every night starting at 11:30 PM. *San Andrés 38, tel. 91/445–3752.*

CAFÉ JAZZ POPULART. Blues, jazz, Brazilian music, reggae, and salsa start at 11 PM. *Huertas 22, tel. 91/429–8407.*

CHOCOLATERÍA SAN GINÉS. Open from 6 PM to 7 AM, this is traditionally the last stop of the bleary-eyed after a hedonistic night out. Stumble in for great cups of thick *chocolate*, crisp *churros*, and a glass of water. *Pasadizo de San Ginés (enter by Arenal 11), tel. 91/365–6546. Closed Mon.*

CLAMORES. This famous jazz club serves a wide selection of French and Spanish champagnes. *Albuquerque 14, tel. 91/445–7938.*

NEGRA TOMASA. Under palm fronds and fishnets, the crowd drinks mojitos (made from sugar, crushed limes, mint, crushed ice, and flavored rum) to horns, maracas, and drums at this Cuban music bar. The house trio draws an international crowd on weekends. *C. Espoz y Mina and C. Cadiz, tel. 91/523–5830.*

SIROCO. The music is live until 12:30 AM Thursday to Saturday; then funk and techno reign until 6 AM. *San Dimas 3, tel. 91/593–3070.*

SURISTAN. This relaxed venue just off the Plaza Santa Ana is a café by day, a college bar by evening, and an avant-garde theater of sorts late at night. It's a hip indie spot for nightly rock and pop concerts, as well as occasional theater and readings. *La Cruz 7, tel. 91/532–3909.*

TORERO. A thoroughly modern club despite its name, Torero is for the beautiful people—quite literally: a bouncer allows only those judged *gente guapa* (beautiful people) to enter. It's one of Madrid's most stylin' spots. *Cruz 26, tel. 91/523–1129.*

THE ARTS

As Madrid's reputation as a vibrant, contemporary arts center has grown, artists and performers of all stripes have arrived in droves. To see what's on, consult the weekly *Guía del Ocio* (published Monday) or daily listings in the leading newspaper, *El País*, both of which are easy to comprehend even if you don't read Spanish. Tickets for the classical performing arts are best purchased at the hall itself; those for major pop concerts are sold at **El Corte Inglés** department stores (tel. 902/400222), **FNAC** (Preciados 28, tel. 91/595–6100), and **Tele-Entradas** (tel. 902/101212).

The city throws major arts festivals in each of the four seasons. The most comprehensive is the Festival de Otoño (Autumn

Festival), from late September to late November, which blankets the entire city with pop concerts, poetry readings, flamenco, and ballet and theater from world-renowned companies. Other annual events include world-class bonanzas of film, contemporary art, and jazz, salsa, rock, and African music, all at very reasonable prices.

Concerts/Ballet

The modern **AUDITORIO NACIONAL DE MÚSICA** (Príncipe de Vergara 146, tel. 91/337–0100, www.auditorionacional.mcu.es) is Madrid's main concert hall, with spaces for both symphonic and chamber music. The resplendent **TEATRO REAL** (Plaza de Isabel II, tel. 91/516–0660) hosts opera and ballet.

The subterranean **CENTRO CULTURAL DE LA VILLA** (Plaza de Colón, tel: 91/575–6080 for information; 91/516–0606 for tickets) has an eclectic program ranging from gospel and blues to flamenco and Celtic dance. The **FUNDACIÓN JUAN MARCH** (Castello 77, tel. 91/435–4240) offers chamber music Monday at noon, Wednesday at 7:30, and Saturday at noon. Both the **CONVENTO DE LA ENCARNACIÓN** and the **REAL ACADEMIA DE BELLAS ARTES DE SAN FERNANDO** host concerts as well.

Film

Nearly a dozen theaters regularly show foreign films, most in English with Spanish subtitles. These are listed in newspapers and in the *Guía de Ocio* under "V.O."—original version, i.e., undubbed. Your best bet for catching a new release is the **MULTICINES IDEAL** (Doctor Cortezo 6, tel. 91/369–2518), where half of the nine theaters are usually showing English-language art films. The excellent, classic V.O. films at the **FILMOTECA CINE DORÉ** (Santa Isabel 3, tel. 91/369–1125) change daily. Two other leading V.O. theaters are right off Plaza de España: **ALPHAVILLE** (Martín de los Heros 14, tel. 91/584–4524) and **RENOIR** (Martín de los Heros 12, tel. 91/541–4100).

Flamenco

Madrid is not a great city for flamenco, but if you won't be traveling south, here are a few possibilities. Note that prices for dinner and a show tend to be very high; you can save money by dining elsewhere and arriving in time for the show. Drinks are usually extra.

CAFÉ DE CHINITAS. It's expensive, but the flamenco dancing here is the best in Madrid. Try to reserve in advance; shows often sell out. Performances are at 10:30 PM Monday through Saturday. Torrija 7, tel. 91/559–5135.

CASA PATAS. Along with tapas, this well-known space offers good, if somewhat touristy, flamenco. Prices are more reasonable than elsewhere. Shows are at 10:30 PM Monday–Thursday, midnight Friday–Sunday. Canizares 10, tel. 91/369–0496.

CORRAL DE LA MORERÍA. Dinner à la carte and well-known visiting flamenco stars accompany the resident dance troupe. Since Morería opened its doors in 1956, celebrities such as Frank Sinatra and Ava Gardner have left their autographed photos for the walls. Shows are daily, from 10:45 PM to 2 AM. Morería 17 (on C. Bailén; cross bridge over C. Segovia and turn right), tel. 91/365–8446.

Theater

English-language plays are rare. When they do come to town, they're staged at any of a dozen venues. One theater you won't need Spanish for is the **TEATRO DE LA ZARZUELA** (Jovellanos 4, tel. 91/524–5400), which specializes in the traditional Spanish operetta known as zarzuela, a kind of bawdy comedy. The **TEATRO ESPAÑOL** (Príncipe 25, tel. 91/429–6297) keeps 17th-century Spanish classics alive.

In This Chapter

Updated by George Semler

side trips

MADRID'S SOPHISTICATION STANDS in vivid contrast to the ancient ways of the historic towns nearby. Less than an hour from downtown are villages whose farm fields may still be plowed by mules. Like urbanites the world over, Madrileños chill out in the countryside, so getaways to the dozens of Castilian hamlets nearby are cherished by travelers and locals alike.

Numbers in the margins correspond to numbers on the Side Trips from Madrid map.

EL ESCORIAL

50 km (31 mi) northwest of Madrid.

Felipe II was one of history's most deeply religious and forbidding monarchs—not to mention one of its most powerful—and the great granite monastery that he had constructed in a remarkable 21 years (1563–84) is an enduring testament to his character. Outside Madrid in the foothills of the Sierra de Guadarrama, the **❶ REAL MONASTERIO DE SAN LORENZO DE EL ESCORIAL** (Royal Monastery of St. Lawrence of Escorial) is severe, rectilinear, and unforgiving—one of the most gigantic yet simple architectural monuments on the Iberian Peninsula.

Felipe built the monastery in the village of San Lorenzo de El Escorial to commemorate Spain's crushing victory over the French at Saint-Quentin on August 10, 1557, and as a final resting place for his all-powerful father, the Holy Roman Emperor Carlos V. He filled the place with treasures as he ruled the largest empire the world has ever seen, knowing all the while that a marble coffin awaited

him in the pantheon deep below. The building's vast rectangle, encompassing 16 courts, is modeled on the red-hot grille upon which St. Lawrence was martyred—appropriate enough, since August 10 was that saint's day. (It's also said that Felipe's troops accidentally destroyed a church dedicated to St. Lawrence during the battle, and he sought to make amends.) Some years ago a Spanish psychohistorian theorized that the building is shaped like a prone woman and is thus an unintended emblem of Felipe's sexual repression. Lo and behold, this thesis provoked several newspaper articles and a rash of other commentary.

El Escorial is easily reached by car, train, bus, or organized tour from Madrid; simply inquire at a travel agency or the appropriate station. The building and its adjuncts—a palace, museum, church, and more—can take hours or even days to tour. Easter Sunday's candelit midnight mass draws crowds, as does the summer tourist season.

The monastery was begun by Juan Bautista de Toledo but finished in 1584 by Juan de Herrera, who would eventually give his name to a major Spanish architectural school. It was completed just in time for Felipe to die here, gangrenous and tortured by the gout that had plagued him for years, in the tiny, sparsely furnished bedroom that resembled a monk's cell more than the resting place of a great monarch. It is in this bedroom—which looks out, through a private entrance, into the royal chapel—that one most appreciates the man's spartan nature. Spain's later Bourbon kings, such as Carlos III and Carlos IV, had clearly different tastes, and their apartments, connected to Felipe's by the Hall of Battles, are far more luxurious.

Perhaps the most interesting part of the entire Escorial is the **PANTEÓN DE LOS REYES** (Royal Pantheon), which contains the body of every king since Carlos I save three—Felipe V (buried at La Granja), Ferdinand VI (in Madrid), and Amadeus of Savoy (in Italy). The body of Alfonso XIII, who died in Rome in 1941, was brought to El Escorial in January 1980. The rulers' bodies lie in 26 sumptuous marble and bronze sarcophagi that line the walls (three of which are empty, awaiting future rulers). Only those queens who bore sons later crowned lie in the same crypt; the others, along with royal sons and daughters who never ruled, lie nearby, in the **PANTEÓN DE LOS INFANTES.** Many of the royal children are in a single circular tomb made of Carrara marble.

Another highlight is the monastery's surprisingly lavish and colorful **LIBRARY,** with ceiling paintings by Michelangelo disciple Pellegrino Tibaldi (1527–96). The imposing austerity of El

el escorial

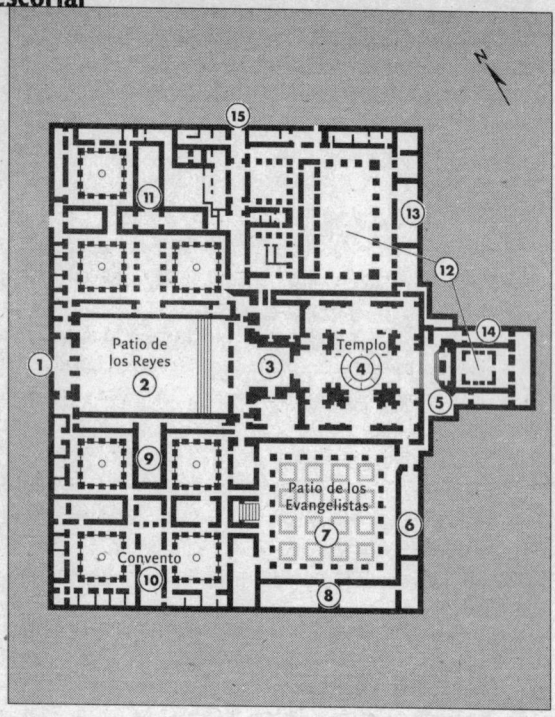

Apartments of Philip II, 14	Convento, 10	Patio de los Reyes (Court of the Kings), 2	Stairway to Panteón de los Reyes (Royal Pantheon), 5
Basilica, 4	Main Entrance, 1	Royal Palace, 12	
Biblioteca (Library), 9	Museum, 13	Sacristy, 6	Tour Entrance, 15
Choir, 3	Patio de los Evangelistas (Court of the Evangelists), 7	Salas Capitulares (Chapter Houses), 8	
Colegio, 11			

Escorial's facades make this chromatic explosion especially powerful; try to save it for last. The library houses 50,000 rare manuscripts, codices, and ancient books, including the diary of St. Teresa of Ávila and the gold-lettered, illuminated Codex Aureus. Tapestries woven from cartoons by Goya, Rubens, and El Greco cover almost every inch of wall space in huge sections of the building, and extraordinary canvases by Velázquez, El Greco, David, Ribera, Tintoretto, Rubens, and other masters, collected from around the monastery, are now displayed in the **MUSEOS NUEVOS** (New Museums). In the **BASILICA**, don't miss the fresco above the choir, depicting heaven, or Titian's fresco *The Martyrdom of St. Lawrence*, which shows the saint being roasted alive. *San Lorenzo de El Escorial, tel. 91/890–5905. 1,000 ptas.; guided tour 1,150 ptas. Apr.–Sept., Tues.–Sun. 10–6; Oct.–Mar., Tues.–Sun. 10–5.*

NEED A BREAK? Many Madrileños find El Escorial the perfect place for an enormous weekend lunch. Topping the list of eating spots is the outdoor terrace at **CHAROLÉS** (Floridablanca 24, tel. 91/890–5975), where imaginative seasonal specialties round out a menu of northern-Spanish favorites, such as *bacalao al pil-pil* (salt cod cooked in oil and garlic at a low temperature) and grilled *chuleta* (steak). Just don't expect picnic prices.

VALLE DE LOS CAÍDOS

2 *13 km (8 mi) north of El Escorial on C600.*

The Valley of the Fallen is just a few minutes north of El Escorial. You drive through a pine-studded state park to this massive basilica, which is carved out of a hill of solid granite and commands magnificent views to the east. Topped with a cross nearly 500 ft high (accessible by elevator), the basilica holds the tombs of both General Franco and José Antonio Primo de Rivera, founder of the Spanish Falange. It was built with the forced labor of Republican prisoners after the civil war and dedicated, rather disingenuously, to all who died in the three-year conflict. The inside recalls *The Wizard of Oz* more than anything else, with every footstep resounding loudly off its stone walls. Tapestries of the Apocalypse add to the generally terrifying air. It's an eerie place for the midnight mass held here on Easter Sunday; the granite peak becomes truly awesome when lit by candlelight. Tel. 91/890–5611. Basilica 750 ptas. Apr.–Sept., Tues.–Sun. 10–7; Oct.–Mar., Tues.–Sun. 10–6.

CHINCHÓN

❸ 54 km (33 mi) southeast of Madrid, off N-III highway on C300.

A true Castilian town, the picturesque village of Chinchón seems a good four centuries removed. It makes an ideal day trip, especially if you save time for lunch at one of its many rustic restaurants; the only problem is that swarms of Madrileños have the same idea, so it's often hard to get a table at lunchtime on weekends.

The high point of Chinchón is its charming **PLAZA MAYOR,** an uneven circle of ancient three- and four-story houses embellished with wooden balconies resting on granite columns. It's something like an open-air Elizabethan theater, but with a Spanish flavor—in fact, the entire plaza is converted to a .bullring from time to time, with temporary bleachers erected in the center and seats on the privately owned balconies rented out for splendid views. (Tickets to these rare fights are hard to come by.) The commanding **IGLESIA DE LA ASUNCIÓN** (Church of the Assumption), overlooking the plaza, is known for its Goya mural, The Assumption of the Virgin.

Along the C300 near the N-III highway, you'll pass through the **VALLE DEL JARAMA,** scene of one of the bloodiest battles of the Spanish Civil War. American volunteers in the Abraham Lincoln Brigade, which fought with the democratically elected Spanish Republican government against Franco's military insurgency, were mauled here in a baptism of fire. Folk singer Pete Seeger immortalized the battle with "There's a valley in Spain called Jarama. . . . " The trenches are still visible, and until recently you could still find bones and rusty military hardware in the fields.

Dining

On winter weekends, Madrileños in droves come for the superb cocido at the **PARADOR DE CHINCHÓN** (Avda. Generalísimo 1, tel. 91/894-0836). The town's arcaded plaza is ringed by charming balconied restaurants serving hearty Castilian fare, particularly roasts and charcoal-grilled meat. **MESÓN DE LA VIRREINA** (Plaza Mayor 28, tel. 91/894-0015), on the square's northeast corner, is a perfect perch for sipping gazpacho or a glass of Chinchón *anís* (anise). Call ahead for a table at **CAFÉ DE LA IBERIA** (Plaza Mayor 17, tel. 91/894-0998), which has a balcony as well as a cozy interior. **MESÓN LAS CUEVAS DEL VINO** (Benito Hortelano 13, tel. 91/894-0206) is a rambling tavern with roaring fireplaces in season, and immense antique wine and olive-oil amphoras scattered around a giant olive press. Wherever you dine, try the local *anís*, a licorice-flavored spirit; and if you come to Chinchón in April, look for merriment occasioned by the Fiesta del Anís y del Vino (Anise and Wine Festival).

MONASTERIO DE EL PAULAR
AND LOZOYA VALLEY

4 *100 km (62 mi) north of Madrid.*

Rising from Spain's great central *meseta* (plain), the Sierra de Guadarrama looms northwest of Madrid like a dark, jagged shield separating Old and New Castile. Snowcapped for much of the year, the mountains are indeed rough-hewn in many spots, particularly on their northern face, but there is a dramatic exception—the Lozoya Valley.

About 100 km (62 mi) north of the capital, this valley of pines, poplars, and babbling brooks is a cool, green retreat from the often searing heat of the plain. Madrileños repair here for a picnic or a simple drive, rarely joined by foreign travelers, to whom the area is virtually unknown.

Smart Sightseeings

Savvy travelers and others who take their sightseeing seriously have skills worth knowing about.

DON'T PLAN YOUR VISIT IN YOUR HOTEL ROOM Don't wait until you pull into town to decide how to spend your days. It's inevitable that there will be much more to see and do than you'll have time for: choose sights in advance.

ORGANIZE YOUR TOURING Note the places that most interest you on a map, and visit places that are near each other during the same morning or afternoon.

START THE DAY WELL EQUIPPED Leave your hotel in the morning with everything you need for the day—maps, medicines, extra film, your guidebook, rain gear, and another layer of clothing in case the weather turns cooler.

TOUR MUSEUMS EARLY If you're there when the doors open you'll have an intimate experience of the collection.

EASY DOES IT See museums in the mornings, when you're fresh, and visit sit-down attractions later on. Take breaks before you need them.

STRIKE UP A CONVERSATION Only curmudgeons don't respond to a smile and a polite request for information. Most people appreciate your interest in their home town. And your conversations may end up being your most vivid memories.

GET LOST When you do, you never know what you'll find—but you can count on it being memorable. Use your guidebook to help you get back on track. Build wandering-around time into every day.

QUIT BEFORE YOU'RE TIRED There's no point in seeing that one extra sight if you're too exhausted to enjoy it.

TAKE YOUR MOTHER'S ADVICE Go to the bathroom when you have the chance. You never know what lies ahead.

You'll need a car to make this trip, and the drive is a pleasant one. Take the A6 northwest from Madrid and exit at signs for the Navacerrada Pass on the N601. As you climb toward the 6,100-ft mountain pass, you'll come to a road bearing off to the left toward Cercedilla. (This little village, a popular base for hikes, is also accessible by train.) Just above Cercedilla, an old Roman road leads up to the ridge of the Guadarrama, where an ancient fountain, known as Fuenfría, long provided the spring water that fed the Roman aqueduct of Segovia. The path traced by this cobble road is very close to the route Hemingway had his hero Robert Jordan take in For Whom the Bell Tolls, and eventually takes you near the bridge that Jordan blew up in the novel.

If you continue past the Cercedilla road, you'll come to a ski resort at the highest point of the Navacerrada Pass. Take a right here on C604 and you'll follow the ridge of the mountains for a few miles before descending into the **LOZOYA VALLEY.**

Looming on your left as you approach the valley floor is the **MONASTERIO DE EL PAULAR** (tel. 91/869–1425). Built by King Juan I in 1390, this was the first Carthusian monastery in Castile, but it has been badly neglected since the Disentailment of 1836, when religious organizations gave their artistic treasures to the state. Fewer than a dozen Benedictine monks still live here, eating and praying exactly as their predecessors did centuries ago. One of them gives tours every day but Thursday at noon, 1, and 5.

The monastery is attached to the hotel **Santa María de El Paular** (tel. 91/869–1011, fax 91/869–1006), a cozy mountain refuge recently acquired and refurbished by the Westin chain.

The valley is filled with picnic spots along the Lozoya River, including several campgrounds. To end the excursion, take C604 north a few miles to Rascafría, and then turn right on a smaller road marked for Miraflores de la Sierra. In that town you'll turn right again, following signs for Colmenar Viejo, and then pick up a short expressway back to Madrid.

In This Chapter

Prices 94

Updated by George Semler

where to stay

SPAIN'S MAJOR PRIVATE HOTEL GROUPS include the Tryp and the NH chain, which is concentrated in major cities like Madrid and which appeals to business travelers. In addition, reasonably priced *hostales* are concentrated in the old city between the Prado and the Puerta del Sol; start your quest around the Plaza Santa Ana. Because they're often full and don't take reservations, we list only a few here—you simply have to go door-to-door and trust your luck.

The Spanish government rates hotels with one to five stars. While quality is a factor, the rating is technically only an indication of how many facilities the hotel offers. For example, a three-star hotel may be just as comfortable as a four-star hotel but lack a swimming pool.

All hotel entrances are marked with a blue plaque bearing the letter H and the number of stars. The letter R (standing for *residencia*) after the letter H indicates an establishment with no meal service. The designations *fonda* (F), *pensión* (P), *hostal* (Hs), and *casa de huéspedes* (CH) indicate budget accommodations.

Although a single room (*habitación sencilla*) is usually available, singles are often on the small side. Solo travelers might prefer to pay a bit extra for single occupancy of a double room (*habitación doble uso individual*). All hotels we review have private bathrooms unless otherwise noted.

Prices

Prices in Madrid are about the same as those in other European capitals. The Ritz, the Palace, and the Villamagna charge upwards of U.S. $400 a night. If that's too steep, try bargaining: because most hotels cater to business travelers, special weekend rates are widely available. You may be able to save 30% on a Friday, Saturday, or Sunday night, and many hotels throw in extras, like meals or museum admissions. Business travelers on long stays can ask for discounts, which can be as deep as 40%. If you're willing to hunt a bit, you can find hostales for 4,000 ptas. or even less. Most of these very cheap rooms are on the upper floors of apartment buildings and share bath facilities.

By law, hotel prices must be posted at the reception desk and should indicate whether or not the value-added tax (IVA; 7%) is included. Breakfast is normally *not* included. Note that high-season rates prevail not only in summer but also during Holy Week and local fiestas.

CATEGORY	COST*
$$$$	over 40,000 ptas./€240
$$$	25,000 ptas.–40,000 ptas./€150–€240
$$	15,000 ptas.–25,000 ptas./€90–€150
$	under 15,000 ptas./€90

for a standard double room, excluding tax

$$$$ ★ **ORFILA.** This elegant 1886 townhouse is hidden away in a leafy little residential street not far from Plaza Colón. It's hard to imagine where you'd be better off in Madrid, as this cozy spot offers every comfort of a larger hotel in an infinitely more intimate, personalized atmosphere. Originally the in-town residence of the eminent literary and aristocratic Gomez-Acebo family, Orfila 6 was an address famous for theater performances in the late 19th and early 20th centuries. The restaurant, garden, and tea room are superbly decorated with period furniture while the guest

rooms are gracefully and luxuriously draped with striped and floral silks. *Orfila 6, 28010, tel. 91/702–7770, fax 91/702–7772. 28 rooms, 4 suites. Restaurant, bar, tea room, in-room VCRs, pool, sauna, health club, meeting room, parking (fee). AE, DC, MC, V.*

$$$$ RITZ. When Alfonso XIII was preparing for his marriage to Queen Victoria's granddaughter, he realized to his dismay that Madrid did not have a single hotel up to the standards of his royal guests. Thus was born the Ritz, and it was long the most exclusive hotel in Spain. Opened in 1910 by the king himself (who had personally overseen its construction), the Ritz is a monument to the Belle Epoque, its sumptuous salons furnished with rare antiques, hand-embroidered linens from Robinson & Cleaver, and handwoven carpets. Guest rooms are carpeted, hung with chandeliers, and decorated in pastels, and many have good views of the Prado or the Castellana. If you can't stay here, try to visit the garden terrace for a drink: the restaurant, Goya is justly famous (though very pricey), and Sunday brunch is a lavish affair to the soothing strains of harp music. Weekend tea and supper are accompanied by chamber music from February to May. Alas, because the lobby and lounge are often crowded with conventioneers and partygoers, the Ritz has lost much of its exclusivity. *Plaza de Lealtad 5, 28014, tel. 91/521–2857, fax 91/701–6776. 158 rooms. Restaurant, bar, in-room data ports, in-room fax, in-room VCRs, hair salon, massage, sauna, health club, parking (fee). AE, DC, MC, V.*

$$$$ SANTO MAURO. Once the Canadian embassy, this turn-of-the-★ 20th-century mansion is now an intimate luxury hotel, an oasis of calm just a 10-minute cab ride from the city center. The neoclassical architecture is accented by contemporary furniture in such hues as mustard, teal, and eggplant. The best rooms are in the main building, as is the top-notch restaurant, which has a contemporary menu and, in season, a delightful dining terrace. Rooms in the new annex are duplexes with stereos and VCRs. Views vary; request a room with a terrace overlooking the gardens. *Zurbano 36, 28010, tel. 91/319–6900, fax 91/308–5477. 37 rooms.*

Restaurant, bar, coffee shop, in-room VCRs, pool, sauna, gym, meeting room, parking (fee). AE, DC, MC, V.

$$$$ VILLA MAGNA. Part of the Park Hyatt group, the Villa Magna is one of Madrid's top luxury hotels, its concrete facade belying an interior furnished with 18th-century antiques. Prices are excessive, but it's hard to find such finishing touches as a champagne bar and—in the largest suite in Madrid—a white baby-grand piano. All rooms have large desks as well as VCRs, and all bathrooms have fresh flowers. One restaurant, Le Divellec, has walnut paneling and the feel of an English library, and you can dine on its garden terrace in season. The other restaurant, the Tse-Yang, is Madrid's most exclusive for Chinese food. The hotel has direct access to a branch of El Corte Inglés department store. *Paseo de la Castellana 22, 28046, tel. 91/587–1234, fax 91/431–2286 or 91/575–3158. 164 rooms, 18 suites. 2 restaurants, 2 bars, in-room VCRs, hair salon, massage, sauna, health club, baby-sitting, business services, car rental, parking (fee). AE, DC, MC, V.*

$$$$ VILLA REAL. For a medium-size hotel that combines elegance, modern amenities, friendly service, and a great location, look no further: the Villa Real faces Spain's parliament and is convenient to almost everything, particularly the Prado and Thyssen-Bornemisza museums. The simulated 19th-century facade gives way to an intimate lobby garnished with potted palms. Each room has its own character—some contemporary, some traditional—and many are split-level, with a small sitting area. Some suites have saunas and whirlpool baths. *Plaza de las Cortés 10, 28014, tel. 91/420–3767, fax 91/420–2547. 94 rooms, 20 suites. Restaurant, bar, in-room data ports, hair salon, sauna, meeting room, parking (fee). AE, DC, MC, V.*

$$$$ WESTIN PALACE. Built in 1912, Madrid's most famous grand
★ hotel is a Belle Epoque creation of Alfonso XIII and has hosted the likes of Dalí, Brando, Hayworth, and Madonna. In 1995 the hotel was acquired by Westin, and by 1998 it had undergone its first

restoration in 85 years. Guest rooms now meet today's highest standards; banquet halls and lobbies have been lovingly beautified; and the facade has been finely restored. The Palace is more charming and stylish than ever—and while the stained-glass dome over the lounge remains exquisitely original, the windows in the guest rooms are now double glazed. The suites are no less luxurious than the opulent public spaces, and bathrooms are spacious, with double sinks, tubs, separate shower stalls, and other welcome touches such as bathrobes and magnifying mirrors. *Plaza de las Cortes 7, 28014, tel. 91/360–8000, fax 91/360–8100, www.palacemadrid.com. 465 rooms, 45 suites. 2 restaurants, bar, café, in-room data ports, sauna, gym, business services, meeting room, parking (fee). AE, DC, MC, V.*

$$$ ★ JARDÍN DE RECOLETOS. This sleek apartment hotel offers great value in a quiet street close to Plaza Colón and upmarket Calle Serrano. The large lobby has marble floors and a stained-glass ceiling, and adjoins a café and restaurant where you can dine or just have drinks beside a tree-lined patio. The commodious rooms, decorated with light-wood trim, white walls, and beige and yellow furnishings, include sitting and dining areas and well-equipped kitchens. "Superior" rooms and two-room suites have hydromassage baths and large terraces. Book well in advance. *Gil de Santivañes 6, 28001, tel. 91/781–1640, fax 91/781–1641. 36 rooms, 7 suites. Restaurant, café, in-room data ports, in-room VCRs, kitchenettes, parking (fee). AE, DC, MC, V.*

$$$ NH LAGASCA. In the heart of the elegant Salamanca neighborhood, this newish hotel combines large, brightly decorated rooms with an unbeatable location two blocks from Madrid's main shopping street, Calle Serrano. The marble lobbies border on the coldly functional, but they're fine as a meeting place. *Lagasca 64, 28001, tel. 91/575–4606, fax 91/575–1694. 100 rooms. Restaurant, bar, in-room VCRs, meeting room, parking (fee). AE, DC, MC, V.*

madrid lodging

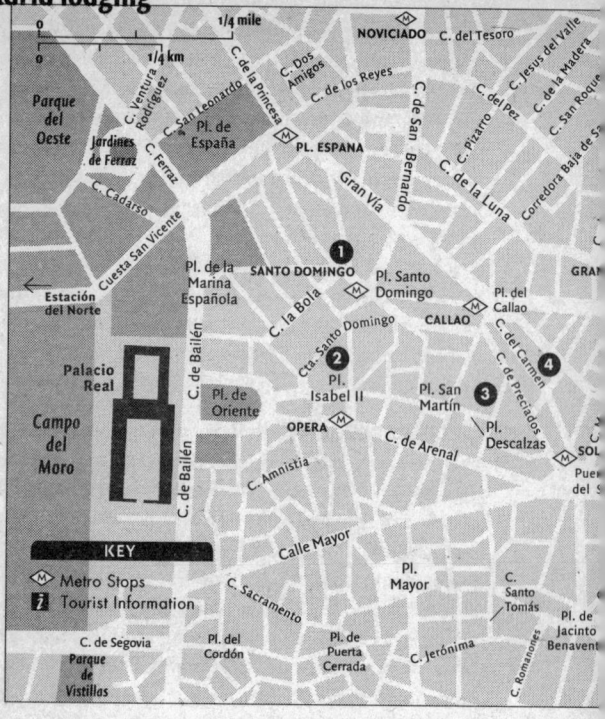

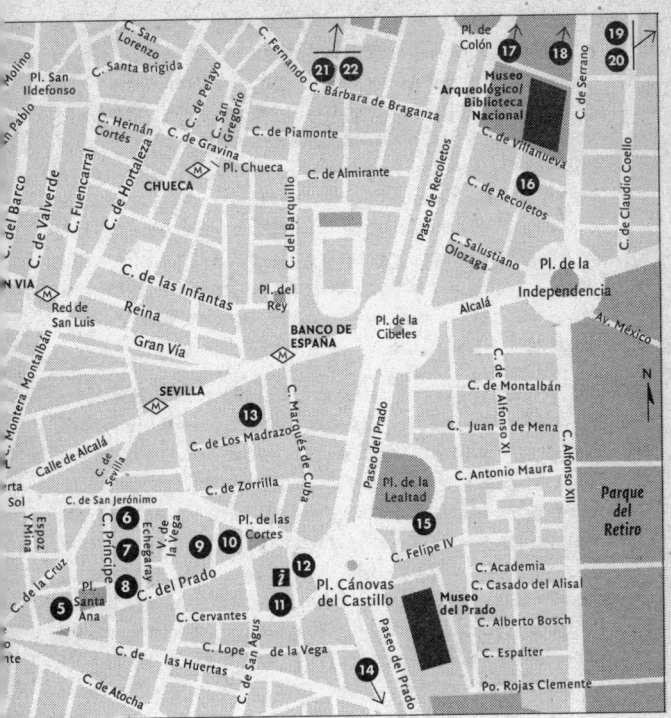

$$$ REINA VICTORIA. Long a Madrid favorite, particularly with bullfighters, this gleaming white Victorian building across Plaza Santa Ana from the Teatro Español was transformed at the end of the 20th century into an upscale modern establishment. The pervasive taurine theme is most evident in the bar, where stuffed bulls' heads peer curiously over your shoulder. The best rooms are the highest, for both the quiet and the views over the rooftops or theater. Two caveats: on Friday and Saturday nights it can be impossible to escape the street noise below, and the coffee in the breakfast room should be avoided at all costs. *Plaza Santa Ana 14, 28012, tel. 91/531–4500, fax 91/522–0307. 195 rooms. Breakfast room, bar, meeting rooms. AE, DC, MC, V.*

$$$ TRYP AMBASSADOR. Ideally located on an old street between Gran
★ Vía and the Royal Palace, the Ambassador occupies the renovated 19th-century palace of the Dukes of Granada. A magnificent front door and a graceful three-story staircase are legacies of the building's aristocratic past; the rest has been transformed into elegant, somewhat soulless lodgings favored by executives. Guest rooms are large, complete with sitting areas, and have mahogany furnishings, floral drapes, and bedspreads. The greenhouse restaurant, filled with plants and songbirds, is especially pleasant on cold days. *Cuesta Santo Domingo 5 and 7, 28013, tel. 91/541–6700, fax 91/559–1040, www.tryp.es. 181 rooms. Restaurant, bar, airport shuttle, parking (fee). AE, DC, MC, V.*

$$$ TRYP FÉNIX. A magnificent marble lobby greets your arrival at this Madrid institution, overlooking Plaza de Colón on the Castellana. The Fénix is also a mere hop from the posh shops of Calle Serrano. Its spacious rooms, decorated in reds and golds, are carpeted and amply furnished, and flowers abound. Ask for a room facing the Plaza de Colón; otherwise, the view is rather dreary. *Hermosilla 2, 28001, tel. 91/431–6700, fax 91/576–0661. 213 rooms, 12 suites. Bar, café, hair salon, baby-sitting, parking (fee). AE, DC, MC, V.*

$$–$$$ SANTO DOMINGO. An intimate hotel that blends the best of classical and modern design, the Santo Domingo is about 10 minutes' walk from the Puerta del Sol, just off Gran Vía. Rooms are decorated in soft tones of peach and ocher, and those on the fifth floor have views of the Royal Palace. All have voice mail and double-paned windows. A friendly staff gives the place a personal touch. *Plaza Santo Domingo 13, 28013, tel. 91/547–9800, fax 91/547–5995. 120 rooms. Restaurant, bar, meeting room, parking (fee). AE, DC, MC, V.*

$$–$$$ SUECIA. The Suecia's chief attraction is its location, right next to the super-chic Círculo de Bellas Artes (an arts society–café–film–theater complex). The large lobby, which includes a café, is often bustling. Guest rooms are trendy, with contemporary art and futuristic light fixtures, but a little worn. *Marqués de Riera 4, 28014, tel. 91/531–6900, fax 91/521–7141. 119 rooms, 9 suites. 2 restaurants, bar, baby-sitting, parking (fee). AE, DC, MC, V.*

$$ CARLOS V. If you like to be in the center of things, hang your hat at this classic hotel on a pedestrian street: it's mere steps from the Puerta del Sol, Plaza Mayor, and Descalzas Reales convent, and the price is right. A suit of armor decorates the tiny lobby, while crystal chandeliers add elegance to the second-floor guest lounge. All rooms are bright and carpeted, and the doubles with large terraces are a bargain. *Maestro Victoria 5, 28013, tel. 91/531–4100, fax 91/531–3761. 67 rooms, 41 with bath. Bar, airport shuttle. AE, DC, MC, V.*

$$ EL PRADO. Wedged between the classic buildings of *castizo* Madrid, this skinny new hotel is within stumbling distance of the city's best bars and nightclubs and is priced accordingly. Rooms are basic but spacious, and virtually immune to street noise thanks to double-pane windows. Decorative touches include pastel floral prints and gleaming marble baths. *C. Prado 11, 28014, tel. 91/369–0234, fax 91/429–2829. 47 rooms. Cafeteria, meeting room, parking (fee). AE, DC, MC, V.*

$$ LIABENY. A large, paneled lobby leads to bars, a restaurant, and a café in this 1960s hotel, centrally located near an airy plaza (and several department stores) between Gran Vía and Puerta del Sol. The large, comfortable rooms have floral fabrics and big windows; interior and top-floor rooms are the quietest. *Salud 3, 28013, tel. 91/531–9000, fax 91/532–5306. 222 rooms. Restaurant, café, 2 bars, meeting room, parking (fee). AE, DC, MC, V.*

$$ SUITE PRADO. Popular with Americans on short stays, this stylish apartment hotel is near the Prado, the Thyssen-Bornemisza, and the Plaza Santa Ana tapas area. The attractive attic studios on the fifth floor have sloping, beamed ceilings, and there are larger suites downstairs. All apartments are brightly decorated and have marble baths and basic kitchens, but breakfast is served by the friendly staff on weekends. *Manuel Fernández y González 10, 28014, tel. 91/420–2318, fax 91/420–0559. 18 suites. Kitchenettes, parking (fee). AE, DC, MC, V.*

$ HOSTAL DULCINEA. Run by an elderly Spanish couple (who also own the Hostal Corbero, across the street), the Dulcinea is a friendly, clean, and affordable alternative to the pricey hotels on Paseo del Prado. Just off the Plaza Cánovas del Castillo, this upper-floor pension has an arguably ideal location: it's surrounded by the Museo Thyssen-Bornemisza to the north, the Prado to the east, and the vibrant nightlife around the Plaza Santa Ana to the west. Rooms are spare, with wood furniture and minimal trimmings, but comfortable and homey. Calling ahead can get you a great price on one of the three cozy "apartments." *Cervantes 19, 28014, tel. 91/429–9309, fax 91/369–2569. 23 rooms, 3 apartments. AE, MC, V.*

$ INGLÉS. Virginia Woolf was among the first luminaries to discover this place, which is smack in the middle of the old city's bar-and-restaurant district. Since Woolf's time, the Inglés has attracted more than its share of less-celebrated artists and writers. Rather drab and deteriorated now, it's best for those looking for location and value rather than luxury. (Run-down suites cost what you'd pay for a standard double.) The balconies overlooking Calle

Echegaray give you an unusual aerial view of the medieval quarter, all red tiles and ramshackle gables. *Echegaray 8, 28014, tel. 91/429–6551, fax 91/420–2423. 58 rooms. Bar, cafeteria, gym, parking (fee).* AE, DC, MC, V.

$ **MORA.** Across the Paseo del Prado from the Botanical Garden,
★ the Mora welcomes weary travelers with a sparkling, faux-marble lobby and bright, carpeted hallways. Guest rooms are modestly decorated but large and comfortable; those on the street side have great views of the gardens and the Prado, and double-pane windows keep them fairly quiet. For breakfast and lunch, the attached café is excellent, affordable, and popular with locals. *Paseo del Prado 32, 28014, tel. 91/420–1569, fax 91/420–0564. 60 rooms. Café.* AE, DC, MC, V.

$ **RAMÓN DE LA CRUZ.** If you don't mind a 10-minute metro ride (to Manuel Becerra) from the city center, this medium-size hotel is a find. Rooms are large, with modern bathrooms, and the stone-floor lobby is spacious. *Don Ramón de la Cruz 94, 28006, tel. 91/401–7200, fax 91/402–2126. 103 rooms. Cafeteria.* MC, V.

PRACTICAL INFORMATION

Air Travel

Several major airlines have regular flights from the United States, and others serve London and other European capitals daily. Shopping among Madrid travel agencies will probably get you a lower fare than those available abroad, especially to and from Great Britain.

BOOKING

When you book **look for nonstop flights** and **remember that "direct" flights stop at least once.** Try to avoid connecting flights, which require a change of plane. For more booking tips and to check prices and make on-line flight reservations, log on to www.fodors.com.

CARRIERS

From North America, American, Continental, US Airways, Air Europa, Spanair, and TWA fly to Madrid; American, Delta, and Iberia fly to Madrid.

The Spanish predilection for cigarettes notwithstanding, most airlines serving Spain, including Iberia, do not allow smoking on either international or domestic flights.

➤ **FROM NORTH AMERICA: Air Europa** (tel. 888/238–7672). **American** (tel. 800/433–7300). **Continental** (tel. 800/231–0856). **Delta** (tel. 800/221–1212). **Iberia** (tel. 800/772–4642). **Spanair** (tel. 888/545–5757). **TWA** (tel. 800/892–4141). **US Airways** (tel. 800/622–1015).

➤ **FROM THE U.K.: British Airways** (tel. 0845/773–3377). **Iberia** (tel. 0845/601–2854).

➤ **WITHIN SPAIN: Iberia** (902/400500). **Air Europa** (tel. 902/401501). **Spanair** (tel. 902/131415).

FLYING TIMES

Flying time from New York is seven hours; from London, just over two hours.

Airport

Madrid is served by Barajas Airport, 12 km (7 mi) east of the city.

➤ **INFORMATION: Aeropuerto de Barajas** (tel. 91/305–8343, 91/305–8344, 91/305–8345, or 91/393–6000).

AIRPORT TRANSFERS

For a mere 475 ptas. there's a convenient bus to the central Plaza Colón, where you can catch a taxi to your hotel. Buses leave every 15 minutes between 5:40 AM and 2 AM (slightly less often very early or late in the day). Watch your belongings, as the underground Plaza Colón bus station is a favorite haunt of purse snatchers and con artists.

The metro is a bargain at 150 ptas. per ticket (or 850 ptas. for a 10-trip ticket that can also be used on city buses), but you have to change trains twice to get downtown, and the trip takes 45 minutes.

In bad traffic, the 15-minute taxi ride to Madrid can take the better part of an hour, but it makes sense if you have substantial luggage. Taxis normally wait outside the airport terminal near the clearly marked bus stop; expect to pay up to 2,500 ptas., more in heavy traffic, plus small holiday, late-night, and/or luggage surcharges. Make sure the driver works on the meter— off-the-meter "deals" almost always cost more. Finally, some hotels offer shuttle service in vans; check with yours when you reserve.

Bus Travel Around Madrid

Red city buses run between 6 AM and midnight and cost 150 ptas. per ride. After midnight, buses called *buyos* (night owls) run out to the suburbs from Plaza de Cibeles for the same price. Signs at every stop list all other stops by street name, but they're hard to comprehend if you don't know the city well. Pick up a free route map from EMT kiosks on the Plaza de Cibeles or the Puerta del Sol, where you can also buy a 10-ride ticket called a Metrobus (850 ptas.) that's valid for the metro. If you speak Spanish, call for information (tel. 91/406–8810).

Drivers will generally make change for anything up to a 2,000-pta. note. If you've bought a 10-ride ticket, step just behind the driver and insert it in the ticket-punching machine until the mechanism rings.

➤ **BUS INFORMATION: City Buses** (tel. 91/406–8810).

Bus Travel

Madrid has no central bus station; buses are generally less popular than trains (though they can be faster). Most of southern Spain is served by the Estación del Sur. Buses for much of the rest of the peninsula, including Cuenca, Extremadura, Salamanca, and Valencia, depart from the Auto Res station. There are several smaller stations, however, so inquire at travel agencies for the one serving your destination.

Bus companies of interest include La Sepulvedana, serving Segovia, Ávila, and La Granja; Herranz, for El Escorial and the Valle de los Caídos; Continental Auto, serving Cantabria and the Basque region; and La Veloz, with service to Chinchón.

For a longer haul, you can travel to Spain by bus from London or Paris. It's a long journey, but the buses are modern, and the fares are a fraction of what you'd pay to fly.

➤ **BUS COMPANIES: Continental Auto** (C. Alenza 20, tel. 91/533–0400; Metro: Ríos Rosas). **Herranz** (Fernández de los Ríos s/n, tel. 91/543–8167; Metro: Moncloa). **La Sepulvedana** (Paseo de la Florida 11, near Estación de Norte, tel. 91/530–4800). **La Veloz** (Mediterraneo 49, tel. 91/409–7602; Metro: Conde de Casal).

➤ **BUS STATIONS: Auto Res** (Plaza Conde de Casal 6, tel. 902/ 020999, metro: Conde de Casal). **Estación del Sur** (Méndez Álvaro s/n, tel. 91/468–4200, metro: Mendez Alvaro).

Business Hours

BANKS & OFFICES

Banks are generally open Monday to Saturday from 8:30 or 9 to 2 or 2:30. In the summer, most close on Saturday. Currency exchanges at airports and train stations stay open later; you can also cash traveler's checks at El Corte Inglés department stores until 9 PM. Most government offices are open weekdays from 9 to 2 only.

MUSEUMS & SIGHTS

Most museums are open from 9:30 to 2 and 4 to 7 six days a week, usually every day but Monday. Schedules are subject to change, of course, particularly between the high and low seasons, so confirm opening hours before you make plans. A few large museums stay open all day, without a siesta.

PHARMACIES

Pharmacies keep normal business hours (9–1:30 and 5–8), but every city neighborhood has a duty pharmacy that stays open 24 hours.

SHOPS

When planning a shopping trip, remember that almost all shops in Spain close at midday for at least three hours. The only exceptions are large supermarkets and the department-store chain El Corte Inglés. Stores are generally open from 9–10 to 1:30 and from 5 to 8. Most shops are closed on Sunday, and in Madrid they're also closed Saturday afternoon. That said, larger shops in tourist areas may stay open Sunday in summer and during the Christmas holiday.

Car Rental

Nearly every international agency is represented in Madrid, whether in town or at Barajas Airport. It's best to reserve a car before you arrive in Spain. Smaller, regional companies offer lower rates. All agencies have a wide range of models, but virtually all cars in Spain have a manual transmission—**if you don't want a stick shift, reserve weeks in advance and specify automatic transmission,** then call to reconfirm your automatic car before you leave for Spain. Rates in Madrid begin at the equivalents of U.S. $65 a day and $300 a week for an economy car with air-conditioning, manual transmission, and unlimited mileage. Add to this a 16% tax on car rentals.

➤ **MAJOR AGENCIES: Alamo** (tel. 800/522–9696; 020/8759–6200 in the U.K.). **Avis** (tel. 800/331–1084; 800/879–2847 in Canada; 02/9353–9000 in Australia; 09/525–1982 in New Zealand; 0870/606–0100 in the U.K.). **Budget** (tel. 800/527–0700). **Dollar** (tel. 800/800–6000). **Europcar** (tel. 0870/607–5000 in the U.K.) **Hertz** (tel. 800/654–3001; 800/263–0600 in Canada; 020/8897–2072 in the U.K.; 02/9669–2444 in Australia; 09/256–8690 in New Zealand). **National** (tel. 800/227–7368; 0208/680–4800 in the U.K.).

➤ **LOCAL AGENCIES: Avis** (tel. 902/135531). **Budget** (tel. 901/201212). **Europcar** (tel. 902/105030). **Hertz** (tel. 902/402405). **National/Atesa** (tel. 902/100101).

INSURANCE

When driving a rented car you are generally responsible for any damage to or loss of the vehicle. Before you rent, see what coverage your personal auto-insurance policy and credit cards provide.

Before you buy collision coverage, check your existing policies—you may already be covered. However, collision policies that car-rental companies sell for European rentals usually do not include stolen-vehicle coverage. Note that in

Italy, all car-rental companies make you buy theft-protection policies.

REQUIREMENTS & RESTRICTIONS

Your own driver's license is valid in Spain, but you may want to get an International Driver's Permit for extra assurance. Permits are available from the American or Canadian automobile association, or, in the United Kingdom, from the Automobile Association or Royal Automobile Club. Note that while anyone over 18 with a valid license can drive in Spain, some rental agencies will not rent cars to drivers under 21.

SURCHARGES

Before you pick up a car in one city and leave it in another, **ask about drop-off charges or one-way service fees,** which can be substantial. Note, too, that some rental agencies charge extra if you return the car before the time specified in your contract. To avoid a hefty refueling fee, **fill the tank just before you turn in the car,** but be aware that gas stations near the rental outlet may overcharge.

Car Travel

Felipe II made Madrid the capital of Spain because it was at the very center of his peninsular domains, and to this day many of the nation's highways radiate from Madrid like the spokes of a wheel. Originating at Kilometer 0—marked by a brass plaque on the sidewalk of the Puerta del Sol—these highways include the A6 (Segovia, Salamanca, Galicia); A1 (Burgos and the Basque Country); the N-II (Guadalajara, Barcelona, France); the N-III (Cuenca, Valencia, the Mediterranean coast); the A4 (Aranjuez, La Mancha, Granada, Seville); the N401 (Toledo); and the N-V (Talavera de la Reina, Portugal). The city is surrounded by the M30 (the inner ring road) and M40 (the outer ring road), from which most of these highways are easily picked up.

Driving in Madrid is best avoided. Parking is nightmarish, traffic is heavy almost all the time, and the city's daredevil drivers can be frightening. August is an exception; the streets are then largely emptied by the mass exodus of Madrileños on vacation.

➤ **LOCAL AUTO CLUBS: RACE** (José Abascal 10, Madrid, tel. 900/200093).

EMERGENCY SERVICES

The rental agencies Hertz and Avis have 24-hour breakdown service. If you belong to an auto club (AAA, CAA, or AA), you can get emergency assistance from their Spanish counterpart, RACE.

GASOLINE

Gas stations are plentiful, and some of those on major routes are open 24 hours. Most stations are self-service, though prices are the same as those at full-service stations. You punch in the amount of gas you want (in pesetas, not in liters), unhook the nozzle, pump the gas, and then pay. At night, however, you must pay before you fill up. Most pumps offer a choice of gas, including leaded, unleaded, and diesel, so **be careful to pick the right one** for your car. All newer cars in Spain use *gasolina sin plomo* (unleaded gas), which is available in two grades, 95 and 98 octane. *Super*, regular 97-octane leaded gas, is gradually being phased out. Prices vary little among stations and were at press time 146 ptas./€.87 a liter for leaded, 97 octane; 135 ptas./€.81 a liter for *sin plomo* (unleaded; 95 octane), and 150 ptas./€.90 a liter for unleaded, 98 octane. Credit cards are widely accepted.

ROAD CONDITIONS

Spain's highway system now includes some 6,000 km (3,600 mi) of beautifully maintained superhighways. Still, you'll find some stretches of major national highways that are only two lanes wide, where traffic often backs up behind slow, heavy trucks. *Autopista* tolls are steep.

Madrid has notoriously long morning and evening rush hours. If possible, **avoid the morning rush hour, which can last until noon, and the evening rush hour, which lasts from 7 to 9.**

RULES OF THE ROAD

Spaniards drive on the right. Horns are banned in cities, but that doesn't keep people from blasting away. Children under 10 may not ride in the front seat, and seat belts are compulsory everywhere. Speed limits are 50 kph (31 mph) in cities, 100 kph (62 mph) on N roads, 120 kph (74 mph) on the *autopista* or *autovía*, and, unless otherwise signposted, 90 kph (56 mph) on other roads.

Spanish highway police are particularly vigilant about speeding and illegal passing. Fines start at 15,000 ptas./€90, and police are empowered to demand payment from non-Spanish drivers on the spot. Although local drivers, especially in cities like Madrid, will park their cars just about anywhere, you should **park only in legal spots.** Parking fines are steep, and your car might well be towed, resulting in fines, hassle, and wasted time.

Children in Spain

Children are greatly indulged in Spain. You'll see kids accompanying their parents everywhere, including bars and restaurants, so bringing yours along should not be a problem. Shopkeepers will shower your child with *caramelos* (sweets), and even the coldest waiters tend to be friendlier when you have a youngster with you. And although you won't be shunted into a remote corner when you bring kids into a Spanish restaurant, you won't find high chairs or special children's menus. Children are expected to eat what their parents do, so it's perfectly acceptable to ask for an extra plate and share your food. Be prepared for late bedtimes, especially in summer—it's common to see toddlers playing cheerfully outdoors until midnight. Because children are expected to be with their parents at all times, few hotels provide baby-sitting services; but those that don't can often refer you to an independent baby-sitter (*canguro*). For general advice about traveling with children consult *Fodor's FYI: Travel with Your Baby* (available in bookstores everywhere).

If you decide to rent a car, **arrange for a car seat when you reserve.**

FOOD

Visiting children may turn up their noses at some of Spain's regional specialties. Although kids seldom get their own menus, most restaurants are happy to provide simple dishes, such as plain grilled chicken, steak, or fried potatoes, for the little ones. *Pescadito frito* (batter-fried fish) is one Spanish dish that most kids do seem to enjoy. If all else fails, familiar fast-food chains such as McDonald's, Burger King, and Pizza Hut are well represented.

SIGHTS & ATTRACTIONS

Museum admissions and bus and metro rides are generally free for children up to age five. We indicate places that children might especially enjoy with a rubber duck (🦆) in the margin.

SUPPLIES & EQUIPMENT

Disposable diapers (*pañales*), formula (*leche maternizada*), and bottled baby foods (*papillas*) are readily available at supermarkets and pharmacies.

Dining

Spaniards love to eat out, and restaurants in Spain have evolved dramatically thanks to a favorable economic climate and burgeoning tourism. A new generation of Spanish chefs—some with international reputations—has transformed classic dishes to suit contemporary tastes, drawing on some of the freshest ingredients in Europe.

The restaurants featured in this book are the cream of the crop in each price range. Restaurants are identified by a crossed knife-and-fork icon (✗); establishments with a (✗🏨) symbol are hotels with restaurants that stand out for their cuisine and are open to nonguests.

HEALTH CONCERNS

At the end of 2000, the first cases of bovine spongiform encephalopathy (BSE, or "mad cow disease") were detected among Spanish cattle, raising questions about the safety of eating beef in Spain. Cattle is subject to testing, and local health authorities have declared it safe to eat Spanish beef and veal, but dishes containing brains or cuts including the spinal cord should be avoided.

Disabilities & Accessibility

Unfortunately, Spain has done little to make traveling easy for visitors with disabilities. Only the Prado and some newer museums, such as the Reina Sofía and Thyssen-Bornemisza, have wheelchair-accessible entrances or elevators. Most of the churches, castles, and monasteries on a sightseer's itinerary involve quite a bit of walking, often on uneven terrain.

Electricity

To use electric equipment from the United States, **bring a converter and adapter.** Spain's electrical current is 220 volts, 50 cycles alternating current (AC); wall outlets take Continental-type plugs, with two round prongs.

If your appliances are dual-voltage you'll need only an adapter. Don't use 110-volt outlets, marked FOR SHAVERS ONLY, for high-wattage appliances such as hair dryers. Most laptop computers operate equally well on 110 and 220 volts, so they require only an adapter.

Embassies

➤ **CONTACTS: Australia** (Plaza del Descubridor Diego de Ordás 3, tel. 91/441–9300). **Canada** (C. Nuñez de Balboa 35, tel. 91/423–3250). **New Zealand** (Plaza de La Lealtad 2, tel. 91/523–0226). **United Kingdom** (C. Fernando el Santo 19, tel. 91/700–8200). **United States** (C. Serrano 75, tel. 91/577–4000).

Emergencies

In any emergency, call tel. 112. Emergency pharmacies are required by law to be open 24 hours a day on a rotating basis; pharmacy windows and the major daily newspapers list the pharmacies open round-the-clock that day.

➤ **MEDICAL CONTACTS: English-speaking-doctor referrals** (Conde de Aranda 7, tel. 91/435–1823). **Hospital La Paz** (Paseo de la Castellana 261, tel. 91/358–2600). **Hospital Ramon y Cajal** (Carretera de Colmenar, Km 9, tel. 91/336–8000). **Hospital 12 de Octubre** (Carretera de Andalucía, Km 5.4, tel. 91/390–8000).

Etiquette & Behavior

The Spanish are very tolerant of foreigners and their strange ways, but you should always behave with courtesy. Be respectful when visiting churches: casual dress is fine if it's not gaudy or unkempt. Spaniards do object to men going bare-chested anywhere other than the beach or poolside, and generally do not look kindly on public displays of drunkenness.

When addressing Spaniards with whom you are not well acquainted, use the formal *usted* rather than the familiar *tu*. For more on language, *see* Language.

BUSINESS ETIQUETTE

Spanish office hours can be confusing to the uninitiated. Some offices stay open more or less continuously from 9 to 3, with a very short lunch break. Others open in the morning, break up the day with a long lunch break of two–three hours, then reopen at 4 or 5 until 7 or 8. Spaniards enjoy a certain notoriety for their lack of punctuality, but this has changed dramatically in recent years: you are expected to show up for meetings on time. Smart dress is the norm.

Spaniards in international fields tend to conduct business with foreigners in English. If you speak Spanish, address new colleagues with the formal *usted* and the corresponding verb conjugations, then follow the lead in switching to the familiar tu once a working relationship has been established.

Gay & Lesbian Travel

Since the end of Franco's dictatorship, the situation for gays and lesbians in Spain has improved dramatically: the paragraph in the Spanish civil code that made homosexuality a crime was repealed in 1978. Violence against gays does occur, but it's generally restricted to the rougher areas of very large cities.

➤ **LOCAL RESOURCES: GaiInform** (Fuencarral 37, 28004 Madrid, tel. 91/523–0070). **Teléfono Rosa** (C. Finlandia 45, Barcelona, tel. 900/601601).

Health

Sunburn and sunstroke are real risks in summertime Spain. On the hottest sunny days, even those who are not normally bothered by strong sun should cover themselves up; carry sunblock lotion; drink plenty of fluids; and limit sun time for the first few days.

If you require medical attention, ask your hotel's front desk for assistance or go to the nearest public Centro de Salud (day hospital); in serious cases, you'll be referred to the regional hospital. Medical care is good in Spain, but nursing is perfunctory, as relatives are expected to stop by and look after inpatients' needs. In some popular destinations, there are volunteer English interpreters on hand.

Spain was recently documented as having the highest number of AIDS cases in Europe. Those applying for work permits will be asked for proof of HIV-negative status.

Holidays

In 2002, Spain's national holidays include January 1, January 6 (Epiphany), March 29 (Good Friday), May 1 (May Day), August 15 (Assumption), October 12 (National Day), November 1 (All

Saints), December 6 (Constitution), December 8 (Immaculate Conception), and December 25.

Madrid holidays include May 2 (Madrid Day), May 15 (St. Isidro), and November 9 (Almudena).

If a public holiday falls on a Tuesday or Thursday, remember that **many businesses also close on the nearest Monday or Friday** for a long weekend called a *puente* (bridge). If a major holiday falls on a Sunday, businesses close on Monday.

Insurance

The most useful travel-insurance plan is a comprehensive policy that includes coverage for trip cancellation and interruption, default, trip delay, and medical expenses (with a waiver for preexisting conditions).

If you're traveling internationally, a key component of travel insurance is coverage for medical bills incurred if you get sick on the road. Such expenses are not generally covered by Medicare or private policies. U.K. residents can buy a travel-insurance policy valid for most vacations taken during the year in which it's purchased (but check preexisting-condition coverage). British and Australian citizens need extra medical coverage when traveling overseas.

Always **buy travel policies directly from the insurance company**; if you buy them from a cruise line, airline, or tour operator that goes out of business you probably will not be covered for the agency or operator's default, a major risk. Before making any purchase, **review your existing health and home-owner's policies** to find what they cover away from home.

➤ **TRAVEL INSURERS: In the U.S.: Access America** (6600 W. Broad St., Richmond, VA 23230, tel. 804/285–3300 or 800/284–8300, www.previewtravel.com), **Travel Guard International** (1145 Clark St., Stevens Point, WI 54481, tel. 715/345–0505 or 800/826–1300, www.noelgroup.com).

➤ **INSURANCE INFORMATION: In the U.K.: Association of British Insurers** (51–55 Gresham St., London EC2V 7HQ, tel. 020/7600–3333, www.abi.org.uk). In Canada: **Voyager Insurance** (44 Peel Center Dr., Brampton, Ontario, L6T 4M8, tel. 905/791–8700, 800/668–4342 in Canada). In Australia: **Insurance Council of Australia** (Level 3, 56 Pitt St., Sydney, NSW 2000, tel. 03/9614–1077). In New Zealand: **Insurance Council of New Zealand** (Box 474, Wellington, tel. 04/472–5230, www.icnz.org.nz).

Language

Although Spaniards exported their language to all Central and South America, you may be surprised to find that Spanish is not the principal language in all of Spain. The Basques speak Euskera; in Catalonia, you'll hear Catalan; in Galicia, Gallego; and in Valencia, Valenciano. Although almost everyone in these regions also speaks and understands Spanish, local radio and television stations may broadcast in these languages, and road signs may be printed (or spray-painted over) with the preferred regional language. Spanish is referred to as Castellano, or Castilian.

Fortunately, Spanish is fairly easy to pick up, and your efforts to speak it will be graciously received. Learn at least the following basic phrases: *buenos días* (hello—until 2 PM), *buenas tardes* (good afternoon—until 8 PM), *buenas noches* (hello—after dark), *por favor* (please), *gracias* (thank you), *adiós* (good-bye), *sí* (yes), *no* (no), *los servicios* (the toilets), *la cuenta* (bill/check), *habla inglés?* (do you speak English?), *no comprendo* (I don't understand).

Lodging

The lodgings we review are the cream of the crop in each price category. We always list the facilities available, but we don't specify whether they cost extra; so when pricing accommodations, always ask what's included and what's not.

Mail & Shipping

Spain's postal system, the *correos*, does work, but delivery times can vary widely. An airmail letter to the United States may take anywhere from four days to two weeks; delivery to other destinations is equally unpredictable. Sending your letters by priority mail ("*urgente*") ensures speedier arrival.

OVERNIGHT SERVICES

When time is of the essence, or when you're sending valuable items or documents overseas, you can use a courier (*mensajero*). The major international agencies, such as Federal Express and UPS, have representatives in Spain; the biggest Spanish courier service is Seur.

➤ **MAJOR SERVICES: DHL** (tel. 902/122424). **Federal Express** (tel. 900/100871). **MRW** (tel. 900/300400). **Seur** (tel. 902/101010). **UPS** (tel. 900/102410).

POSTAL RATES

Airmail letters to the United States and Canada cost 120 ptas./€.72 up to 20 grams. Letters to the United Kingdom and other EU countries cost 75 ptas./€.45 up to 20 grams. Letters within Spain are 40 ptas./€.24. Postcards carry the same rates as letters. You can buy stamps at post offices and at licensed tobacco shops.

RECEIVING MAIL

Because mail delivery in Spain can often be slow and unreliable, it's best to have your mail sent to American Express. Mail can also be held at a Spanish post office; have it addressed to **Lista de Correos** (the equivalent of Poste Restante) in a town you'll be visiting. Postal addresses should include the name of the province in parentheses, e.g., Marbella (Málaga).

➤ **INFORMATION: In the U.S., call American Express** (tel. 800/528–4800) for a list of offices overseas.

Metro Travel

The metro is quick, frequent, and, at 150 ptas. no matter how far you travel, cheap. Even cheaper is the 10-ride Metrobus ticket, or *billete de diez*, which costs 850 ptas., is also valid for buses, and is accepted by automatic turnstiles (lines at ticket booths can be long). The system is open from 6 AM to 1:30 AM, though a few entrances close earlier. There are 10 metro lines, and system maps in every station detail their color-coded routes. Note the end station of the line you need, and just follow signs to the correct corridor. Exits are marked SALIDA.

Money Matters

Spain is no longer a budget destination, but prices still compare slightly favorably with those elsewhere in Europe. Coffee in a bar generally costs 125 ptas./€.75 (standing) or 150 ptas./€.90 (seated). Beer in a bar: 125 ptas./€.75 standing, 150 ptas./€.90 seated. Small glass of wine in a bar: 100 ptas.–150 ptas./€.60–€.90. Soft drink: 150 ptas.–200 ptas./€.90–€1.20 a bottle. Ham-and-cheese sandwich: 300 ptas.–450 ptas./€1.80–€2.70. Two-km (1-mi) taxi ride: 400 ptas./€2.40, but the meter keeps ticking in traffic jams. Local bus or subway ride: 135 ptas.–200 ptas./€.81–€1.20. Movie ticket: 500 ptas.–800 ptas./€3–€4.80 Foreign newspaper: 300 ptas./€1.80. In this book we quote prices for adults only, but note that children, students, and senior citizens almost always pay reduced fees. For information on taxes in Spain, *see* Taxes.

➤ **REPORTING LOST CARDS: American Express** (tel. 900/941413). **Diners Club** (tel. 901/101011). **MasterCard** (tel. 900/974445). **Visa** (tel. 900/971231).

CURRENCY

On January 1, 2002, the European monetary unit, the Euro (€) goes into circulation in Spain and the other countries that have adopted it (Austria, Belgium, Finland, France, Germany, Ireland, Italy, Luxembourg, the Netherlands, and Portugal). To ease the transition, Spanish pesetas will be accepted until March 1, 2002. Euro notes come in denominations of 5, 10, 20, 50, 100, 200, and 500; coins are worth 1 cent of a Euro, 2 cents, 5 cents, 10 cents, 20 cents, 50 cents, 1 Euro, and 2 Euros. At press time, exchange rates were extremely favorable for most English-speaking travelers: €.9 to the U.S. dollar, €.63 to the pound sterling, €1.41 to the Canadian dollar, €1.83 to the Australian dollar, €2.22 to the New Zealand dollar, and €7.25 to the South African rand.

CURRENCY EXCHANGE

For the most favorable rates, **change money through banks.** Although ATM transaction fees may be higher abroad than at home, ATM rates are excellent because they are based on wholesale rates offered only by major banks. You won't do as well at exchange booths in airports or rail and bus stations, in hotels, in restaurants, or in stores. To avoid lines at airport exchange booths, **get a bit of Spanish currency before you leave home.**

Packing

Pack light. Although baggage carts are free and plentiful in most Spanish airports, they're rare in train and bus stations.

On the whole, Spaniards dress up more than Americans or the British. Summer is hot nearly everywhere; visits in winter, fall, and spring call for warm clothing and, in winter, boots. It makes sense to wear casual, comfortable clothing and shoes for sightseeing, but you'll want to **dress up a bit in large cities, especially for fine restaurants and nightclubs.** American tourists are easily spotted for their sneakers—if you want to blend in, wear leather shoes.

Passports & Visas

Visitors from the United States, Australia, Canada, New Zealand, and the United Kingdom need a valid passport to enter

Spain. Australians who wish to stay longer than a month also need a visa, available from the Spanish Embassy in Canberra.

Before you leave home, **make two photocopies of the data page**—one for someone at home and another for you, carried separately from your passport. If you lose your passport, promptly call the nearest embassy or consulate and the local police.

Safety

Petty crime is a huge problem in Madrid. The most frequent offenses are pickpocketing and theft from cars. We cannot overemphasize the fact that you should **never, ever leave anything valuable in a parked car**, no matter how friendly the area feels, how quickly you'll return, or how invisible the item seems once you lock it in the trunk. Thieves can spot rental cars a mile away, and they work very efficiently. In airports, laptop computers are choice prey.

WOMEN IN SPAIN

The traditional Spanish custom of the *piropo* (a shouted "compliment" to women walking down the street) is fast disappearing, though women traveling alone may still encounter it on occasion. The piropo is harmless, if annoying, and should simply be ignored.

Senior-Citizen Travel

Although there are few early bird specials or movie discounts in Spain, senior citizens generally enjoy discounts at museums. Spanish social life encompasses all ages—it's very common to see seniors next to young couples or families in late-night cafés.

To qualify for age-related discounts, **mention your senior status up front** when booking hotel reservations (not when checking out) and before you're seated in restaurants (not when paying the bill). When renting a car, ask about promotional car-rental discounts, which can be cheaper than senior-citizen rates.

Sightseeing Tours

Your hotel can arrange standard city tours in either English or Spanish; most offer Madrid Artístico (including the Royal Palace and the Prado), Madrid Panorámico (a basic half-day tour), Madrid de Noche (including a flamenco or nightclub show), and the Sunday-only Panorámico y Toros (a brief city overview followed by a bullfight). The Plaza Mayor tourist office leads tours of Madrid's old quarters in English every Saturday morning, departing from the office at 10. The same office has a leaflet detailing the popular Spanish-language bus and walking tours run by the *ayuntamiento* (city hall) under the rubric "Descubre Madrid"; you then buy tickets at the Patronato de Turismo. The walking tours, which depart most mornings, visit many hidden corners as well as major sights; theme options include "Medicine in Madrid," "Goya's Madrid," and "Commerce and Finance in Madrid." For day trips to sites outside Madrid, such as Toledo, El Escorial, and Segovia, contact Julià Tours.

Trapsatur runs the *Madrid Visión* tourist bus, which makes a 1½-hour circuit of the city with recorded commentary in English. No reservation is needed; just show up at Gran Vía 32 or the front of the Prado Museum. Buses depart every 1½ hours beginning at 12:30 Monday–Saturday, 10:30 on Sunday. A round-trip ticket costs 1,500 ptas.; a day pass, which allows you to get on and off at various attractions, is 2,000 ptas. An identical hop-on, hop-off service on an open-top double decker is operated by Sol Pentours, whose daily 1½-hour tours leave every half hour from Plaza de España, in front of the Crowne Plaza Hotel, between 10 AM and 8 PM. The fare is 1,600 ptas. Contact the Asociación Profesional de Informadores to hire a personal guide.

➤ **CONTACTS: Asociación Profesional de Informadores** (C. Ferraz 82, tel. 91/542–1214 or 91/541–1221). **Ayuntamiento** (City Hall; C. Mayor 69, tel. 91/588–2900). **Julià Tours** (Gran Vía 68, tel. 91/559–9605). **Patronato de Turismo** (C. Mayor 69, tel. 91/588–

2900). **Plaza Mayor tourist office** (Plaza Mayor 3, tel. 91/588–2900). **Sol Pentours** (Gran Vía 26, tel. 902/303903). **Trapsatur** (tel. 91/302–6039).

Taxes

VALUE-ADDED TAX

Value-added tax, similar to sales tax, is called IVA in Spain (pronounced *"ee-vah"*; for *impuesto sobre el valor añadido*). It is levied on both products and services such as hotel rooms and restaurant meals. When in doubt about whether tax is included, ask, *"Está incluido el IVA"*?

The IVA rate for hotels and restaurants is 7%, regardless of their number of stars or forks. A special tax law for the Canary Islands allows hotels and restaurants there to charge 4% IVA. Menus will generally say at the bottom whether tax is included (*IVA incluido*) or not (*más 7% IVA*).

Whereas food, pharmaceuticals, and household items are taxed at the lowest rate, most consumer goods are taxed at 16%. A number of shops, particularly large stores and boutiques in holiday resorts, participate in Global Refund (formerly Europe Tax-Free Shopping), a V.A.T. refund service that makes getting your money back relatively hassle-free. On purchases of more than 15,000 ptas./€90, you're entitled to a refund of the 16% tax. **Ask for the Global Refund form** (called a Shopping Cheque) in participating stores. You show your passport and fill out the form; the vendor then mails you the refund, or—often more convenient—you **present your original receipt to the VAT office at the airport** when you leave Spain. (In both Madrid and Barcelona, the office is near the duty-free shops. Save time for this process, as lines can be long.) Customs signs the original and refunds your money on the spot in cash (pesetas), or sends it to their central office to process a credit-card refund. Credit-card refunds take a few weeks.

➤ **V.A.T. REFUNDS: Global Refund** (99 Main St., Suite 307, Nyack, NY 10960, tel. 800/566–9828, www.globalrefund.com).

Taxis

Taxis are one of Madrid's few truly good deals. Meters start at 200 ptas. and add 130 ptas. per km (½ mi) thereafter (150 ptas. per km at night, on weekends and holidays, and beyond city limits). Numerous supplemental charges, however, mean that your total cost often bears little resemblance to what you see on the meter. Supplemental charges—over and above your fare—include 150 ptas. on Sundays and holidays and between 11 PM and 6 AM, 150 ptas. to sports stadiums or the bullring, and 450 ptas. (plus 50 ptas. per suitcase) to or from the airport.

Taxi stands are numerous, and taxis are easily hailed in the street—except when it rains, at which point they're exceedingly hard to come by. Available cabs display a LIBRE sign during the day, a green light at night. Spaniards do not tip cabbies, but if you're inspired, 25 ptas. is about right for shorter rides; you can go as high as 10% for a trip to the airport. You can call a cab through Tele-Taxi, Radioteléfono Taxi, or Radio Taxi Gremial.

➤ **TAXIS AND SHUTTLES: Radio Taxi Gremial** (tel. 91/447–5180). **Radioteléfono Taxi** (tel. 91/547–8200). **Tele-Taxi** (tel. 91/371–2131).

Telephones

Spain's phone system is perfectly efficient. Direct dialing is the norm. The main operator is Telefónica. Note that only cell phones conforming to the European GSM standard will work in Spain.

AREA & COUNTRY CODES

The country code for Spain is 34. Phoning home: country codes are 1 for the United States and Canada, 44 for the United Kingdom, 61 for Australia, and 64 for New Zealand.

DIRECTORY & OPERATOR ASSISTANCE

For general information in Spain, dial 1003. International operators, who generally speak English, are at 025.

INTERNATIONAL CALLS

International calls are awkward from coin-operated pay phones because of the enormous number of coins needed; and they can be expensive from hotels, as the hotel often adds a hefty surcharge. The best way to phone home is to use a public phone that accepts phone cards or go to the local telephone office, the *locutorio*. You converse in a quiet, private booth, and you're charged according to the meter. If the call ends up costing 500 ptas./€3 or more, you can pay with Visa or MasterCard.

To make an international call yourself, dial 00, then the country code, then the area code and number.

Madrid's main telephone office is at Gran Vía 28. There's another at the main post office, and a third at Paseo Recoletos 43, just off Plaza Colón. In Barcelona you can phone overseas from the office at Carrer de Fontanella 4, off Plaça de Catalunya.

Before you leave home, **find out your long-distance company's access code in Spain.**

LOCAL CALLS

All area codes begin with a 9. To call within Spain—even locally—dial the area code first. Numbers preceded by a 900 code are toll-free; those starting with a 6 are going to a cellular phone. Note that calls to cell phones are significantly more expensive than calls to regular phones.

LONG-DISTANCE SERVICES

AT&T, MCI, and Sprint access codes make calling long distance relatively convenient, but you may find the local access number blocked in many hotel rooms. First ask the hotel operator to connect you. If the hotel operator can't comply, ask for an international operator, or dial the international operator yourself. One way to improve your odds of getting connected to your long-distance carrier is to travel with more than one company's calling card (a hotel may block Sprint, for example, but not MCI). If all else fails, call from a pay phone.

➤ **GENERAL INFORMATION: AT&T** (tel. 800/222–0300). **MCI WorldCom** (tel. 800/444–4444). **Sprint** (tel. 800/793–1153).

➤ **ACCESS CODES IN SPAIN: AT&T** (tel. 900/990011). **MCI** (tel. 900/990014). **Sprint** (tel. 900/990013).

PHONE CARDS

To use a newer pay phone you need a special phone card (*tarjeta telefónica*), which you can buy at any tobacco shop or newsstand, in various denominations. Some such phones also accept credit cards, but phone cards are more reliable.

PUBLIC PHONES

You'll find pay phones in individual booths, in special telephone offices (*locutorios*), and in many bars and restaurants. Most have a digital readout so you can see your money ticking away. If you're calling with coins, you need at least 25 ptas./€.15 to call locally, 75 ptas./€.45 to call another province. Simply insert the coins and wait for a dial tone. (With older models, you line coins up in a groove on top of the dial and they drop down as needed.)

Time

Spain is on Central European Time, one hour ahead of Greenwich Mean Time, six hours ahead of Eastern Standard Time. Like the rest of the European Union, Spain switches to daylight saving time on the last weekend in March, and switches back on the last weekend in October.

Tipping

Waiters and other service staff expect to be tipped, and you can be sure that your contribution will be appreciated. On the other hand, if you experience bad or surly service, don't feel obligated to leave a tip.

Restaurant checks almost always include a service charge, which is not the same as a voluntary tip. **Do not tip more than 10% of the bill,** and leave less if you eat tapas or sandwiches at a bar—just enough to round out the bill to the nearest 100 ptas./€1. Tip cocktail servers 50 ptas.–75 ptas./€.30–€.50 a drink, depending on the bar.

Tip taxi drivers about 10% of the total fare, plus a supplement for a long ride or extra help with luggage. Note that rides from airports carry an official surcharge plus a small handling fee for each piece of luggage.

Tip hotel porters 100 ptas./€.50 a bag, and the bearer of room service 100 ptas./€.50. A doorman who calls a taxi for you gets 100 ptas./€.50. If you stay in a hotel for more than two nights, tip the maid about 100 ptas./€.50 per night. The concierge should receive a tip for any additional help he or she provides.

Tour guides should be tipped about 300 ptas./€2, ushers in theaters or at bullfights 25 ptas.–50 ptas./€.15–€.20, barbers 100 ptas./€.50, and women's hairdressers at least 200 ptas./€1 for a wash and style. Rest-room attendants are tipped 25 ptas./€.15.

Tours & Packages

Because everything is prearranged on a prepackaged tour or independent vacation, you spend less time planning—and often get it all at a good price.

Don't confuse packages and guided tours. When you buy a package, you travel on your own, just as though you had planned the trip yourself. Fly/drive packages, which combine airfare and car rental, are often a good deal. If you **buy a rail/drive pass,** you may save on train tickets and car rentals. All Eurail- and Europass holders get a discount on Eurostar fares through the Channel Tunnel.

BOOKING WITH AN AGENT

Travel agents are excellent resources. But it's a good idea to collect brochures from several agencies as some agents' suggestions may be influenced by relationships with tour and package firms that reward them for volume sales. If you have a special interest, **find an agent with expertise in that area**; ASTA (☞ Travel Agencies) has a database of specialists worldwide.

Make sure your travel agent knows the accommodations and other services of the place they're recommending. Ask about the hotel's location, room size, beds, and whether it has a pool, room service, or programs for children, if you care about these. Has your agent been there in person or sent others whom you can contact?

Do some homework on your own, too: local tourism boards can provide information about lesser-known and small-niche operators, some of which may sell only direct.

BUYER BEWARE

Each year consumers are stranded or lose their money when tour operators—even large ones with excellent reputations—go out of business. So **check out the operator**. Ask several travel agents about its reputation, and try to **book with a company that has a consumer-protection program.** (Look for information in the company's brochure.) In the United States, members of the National Tour Association and the United States Tour Operators Association are required to set aside funds to cover your payments and travel arrangements in the event that the company defaults. It's also a good idea to choose a company that participates in the American Society of Travel Agents' Tour Operator Program (TOP); ASTA will act as mediator in any disputes between you and your tour operator.

Remember that the more your package or tour includes the better you can predict the ultimate cost of your vacation. Make sure you know exactly what is covered, and **beware of hidden** costs. Are taxes, tips, and transfers included? Entertainment and excursions? These can add up.

➤ **TOUR-OPERATOR RECOMMENDATIONS: American Society of Travel Agents** (☞ Travel Agencies). **National Tour Association** (NTA; 546 E. Main St., Lexington, KY 40508, tel. 859/226–4444 or 800/682–8886, www.ntaonline.com). **United States Tour Operators Association** (USTOA; 342 Madison Ave., Suite 1522, New York, NY 10173, tel. 212/599–6599 or 800/468–7862, www.ustoa.com).

Train Travel

For train schedules and reservations, go to any of Madrid's major train stations, visit a travel agent, or simply call RENFE toll-free. You can charge tickets to your credit card, and even have them delivered to your hotel.

Madrid has three main train stations: Chamartín, Atocha, and Norte, the latter primarily for commuter trains. Remember to confirm which station you need when arranging a trip. Generally speaking, Chamartín, near the northern tip of Paseo de la Castellana, serves points north and west, including Barcelona, San Sebastián, Burgos, León, Oviedo, La Coruña, and Salamanca, as well as France and Portugal. Atocha, at the southern end of Paseo del Prado, serves towns near Madrid, including El Escorial, Segovia, and Toledo, and southern and eastern cities such as Seville, Málaga, Córdoba, Valencia, and Castellón. Atocha also sends AVE (high-speed) trains to Córdoba and Seville.

➤ **TRAIN INFORMATION: Estación de Atocha** (tel. 91/328–9020). **Estación Chamartín** (tel. 91/315–9976). **RENFE** (tel. 902/240202, www.renfe.es/ingles).

Travel Agencies

Scattered throughout Madrid, travel agencies are generally the best way to get tickets, cheap deals, and information without hassles. The major agents below are in central locations. Madrid

& Beyond is a British-run agency that can make all your travel and lodging arrangements in Madrid, other historic cities, and some lovely rural areas.

A good travel agent puts your needs first. Look for an agency that has been in business at least five years, emphasizes customer service, and has someone on staff who specializes in your destination. In addition, make sure the agency belongs to a professional trade organization. If a travel agency is also acting as your tour operator, *see* Buyer Beware in Tours & Packages.

➤ **AGENTS IN MADRID: American Express** (Plaza de las Cortés 2, tel. 91/322–5500). **Carlson Wagons-Lits** (Paseo de la Castellana 96, tel. 91/563–1202). **Madrid & Beyond** (Gran Vía 59-8D, tel. 91/758–0063, fax 91/542–4391). **Pullmantur** (Plaza de Oriente 8, tel. 91/541–1807).

➤ **LOCAL AGENT REFERRALS: American Society of Travel Agents** (ASTA; tel. 800/965–2782 24-hr hot line, www.astanet.com). **Association of British Travel Agents** (68–71 Newman St., London W1T 3AH, U.K., tel. 020/7637–2444, www.abtanet.com). **Association of Canadian Travel Agents** (130 Albert St., Suite 1705, Ottawa, Ontario K1P 5G4, Canada, tel. 613/237–3657, www.acta.net). **Australian Federation of Travel Agents** (Level 3, 309 Pitt St., Sydney, NSW 2000, Australia, tel. 02/9264–3299, www.afta.com.au). **Travel Agents' Association of New Zealand** (Box 1888, Wellington 10033, New Zealand, tel. 04/499–0104, www.taanz.org.nz).

Visitor Information

Madrid has four regional tourist offices. The best is at Duque de Medinaceli 2 (near the Palace hotel), open weekdays 9–7 and Saturday 9–1. The others are at Barajas Airport, open weekdays 9–7 and Saturday 9:30–1:30; the Chamartín train station, open weekdays 8–8 and Saturday 9–1; and the remote Mercado de la Puerta de Toledo, open weekdays 9–7 and Saturday 9–1. The city tourist office on the Plaza Mayor is good for little save a few pamphlets; it's open weekdays 10–8, Saturday 10–2, and Sunday 10–2.

➤ **CITY TOURIST OFFICE: Plaza Mayor 3** (tel. 91/588–1636).

➤ **REGIONAL TOURIST OFFICES: Duque de Medinaceli 2** (tel. 91/429–4951). **Barajas** (tel. 91/305–8656). **Chamartín** (tel. 91/315–9976). **Mercado de la Puerta de Toledo** (Glorieta Puerta de Toledo, 3rd floor, tel. 91/364–1876).

Web Sites

Do check out the World Wide Web when planning your trip. You'll find everything from weather forecasts to virtual tours of famous cities. Be sure to visit **Fodors.com** (www.fodors.com), a complete travel-planning site. You can research prices and book plane tickets, hotel rooms, rental cars, vacation packages, and more. In addition, you can post your pressing questions in the Travel Talk section. Other planning tools include a currency converter and weather reports, and there are loads of links to travel resources.

For more information on Spain, visit the Tourist Office of Spain at www.tourspain.es and see www.okspain.es, www.cyberspain.com, or www.red2000.com/spain.

When to Go

May and October are the optimal times to come to Spain, as the weather is generally warm and dry. May gives you more hours of daylight, while October offers a chance to enjoy the harvest season, which is especially colorful in the wine regions.

In April you can see some of Spain's most spectacular fiestas, particularly Semana Santa (Holy Week); and by then the weather in southern Spain is warm enough to make sightseeing comfortable.

Spain is the number-one destination for European travelers, so if you want to avoid crowds, come before June or after September. Crowds and prices increase in the summer, especially along the coasts, as the Mediterranean is usually too cold for swimming the rest of the year, and beach season on the Atlantic coast is shorter still. Spaniards vacation in August, and their migration to the beach causes huge traffic jams on August 1 and 31. Major cities are relaxed and empty for the duration; small shops and some restaurants shut down for the entire month, but museums remain open.

CLIMATE

Summers in Spain are hot: temperatures frequently hit 100°F (38°C), and air-conditioning is not widespread. Try to **limit summer sightseeing to the morning hours.** That said, warm summer nights are among Spain's quiet pleasures.

Winters in Spain are mild and rainy along the coasts, especially in Galicia. Elsewhere, winter blows bitterly cold. Snow is infrequent except in the mountains, where you can ski from December to March in the Pyrenees and other resorts near Granada, Madrid, and Burgos.

➤ **FORECASTS: Weather Channel Connection** (tel. 900/932–8437), 95¢ per minute from a Touch-Tone phone.

The following are average daily maximum and minimum temperatures for some major Spanish cities.

MADRID

Jan.	48F	9C	May	70F	21C	Sept.	77F	25C
	36	2		50	10		57	14
Feb.	52F	11C	June	81F	27C	Oct.	66F	19C
	36	2		59	15		50	10
Mar.	59F	15C	July	88F	31C	Nov.	55F	13C
	41	5		63	17		41	5
Apr.	64F	18C	Aug.	86F	30C	Dec.	48F	9C
	45	7		63	17		36	2

WORDS AND PHRASES

Basics

ENGLISH	SPANISH	PRONUNCIATION
Yes/no	Sí/no	see/no
Please	Por favor	pohr fah-vohr
May I?	¿Me permite?	meh pehr-mee-teh
Thank you (very much)	(Muchas) gracias	(moo-chas) grah-see-as
You're welcome	De nada	deh nah-dah
Excuse me	Con permiso/ perdón	con pehr-mee-so/ pehr-dohn
Pardon me/ what did you say?	¿Perdón?/Mande?	pehr-dohn/mahn-deh
Could you tell me . . . ?	¿Podría decirme . . . ?	po-dree-ah deh-seer-meh
I'm sorry	Lo siento	lo see-en-to
Good morning!	¡Buenos días!	bway-nohs dee-ahs
Good afternoon!	¡Buenas tardes!	bway-nahs tar-dess
Good evening!	¡Buenas noches!	bway-nahs no-chess
Goodbye!	¡Adiós!/ ¡Hasta luego!	ah-dee-ohss/ ah-stah-lwe-go
Mr./Mrs.	Señor/Señora	sen-yor/sen-yohr-ah
Miss	Señorita	sen-yo-ree-tah
Pleased to meet you	Mucho gusto	moo-cho goose-to
How are you?	¿Cómo está usted?	ko-mo es-tah oo-sted
Very well, thank you.	Muy bien, gracias.	moo-ee bee-en, grah-see-as
And you?	¿Y usted?	ee oos-ted
Hello (on the phone)	Diga	dee-gah

Numbers

1	un, uno	oon, oo-no
2	dos	dohs
3	tres	tress
4	cuatro	kwah-tro
5	cinco	sink-oh
6	seis	saice
7	siete	see-et-eh
8	ocho	o-cho
9	nueve	new-eh-veh
10	diez	dee-es
11	once	ohn-seh
12	doce	doh-seh
13	trece	treh-seh
14	catorce	ka-tohr-seh
15	quince	keen-seh
16	dieciséis	dee-es-ee-saice
17	diecisiete	dee-es-ee-see-et-eh
18	dieciocho	dee-es-ee-o-cho
19	diecinueve	dee-es-ee-new-ev-eh
20	veinte	vain-teh
21	veinte y uno/ veintiuno	vain-te-oo-noh
30	treinta	train-tah
32	treinta y dos	train-tay-dohs
40	cuarenta	kwah-ren-tah
50	cincuenta	seen-kwen-tah
60	sesenta	sess-en-tah
70	setenta	set-en-tah
80	ochenta	oh-chen-tah
90	noventa	no-ven-tah
100	cien	see-en
200	doscientos	doh-see-en-tohss
500	quinientos	keen-yen-tohss
1,000	mil	meel
2,000	dos mil	dohs meel

Days of the Week

Sunday	domingo	doh-meen-goh
Monday	lunes	loo-ness
Tuesday	martes	mahr-tess
Wednesday	miércoles	me-air-koh-less
Thursday	jueves	hoo-ev-ess
Friday	viernes	vee-air-ness
Saturday	sábado	sah-bah-doh

Useful Phrases

Do you speak English?	¿Habla usted inglés?	ah-blah oos-ted in-glehs
I don't speak Spanish	No hablo español	no ah-bloh es-pahn-yol
I don't understand (you)	No entiendo	no en-tee-en-doh
I understand (you)	Entiendo	en-tee-en-doh
I don't know	No sé	no seh
I am American/ British	Soy americano (americana)/ inglés(a)	soy ah-meh-ree-kah-no (ah-meh-ree-kah-nah)/in-glehs(ah)
My name is . . .	Me llamo . . .	meh yah-moh
Yes, please/ No, thank you	Sí, por favor/ No, gracias	see pohr fah-vor/ no grah-see-ahs
Yesterday/today/ tomorrow	Ayer/hoy/mañana	ah-yehr/oy/mahn-yah-nah
This morning/ afternoon	Esta mañana/tarde	es-tah mahn-yah-nah/tar-deh
Tonight	Esta noche	es-tah no-cheh
This/Next week	Esta semana/ la semana que entra	es-tah seh-mah-nah/lah seh-mah-nah keh en-trah
This/Next month	Este mes/el próximo mes	es-teh mehs/el prok-see-moh mehs
How?	¿Cómo?	koh-mo

When?	¿Cuándo?	kwahn-doh
What?	¿Qué?	keh
What is this?	¿Qué es esto?	keh es es-toh
Why?	¿Por qué?	por keh
Who?	¿Quién?	kee-yen
Where is . . . ?	¿Dónde está . . . ?	dohn-deh es-tah
the train station?	la estación del tren?	la es-tah-see-on del train
the subway station?	la estación del metro?	la es-ta-see-on del meh-tro
the bus stop?	la parada del autobus?	la pah-rah-dah del oh-toh-boos
the bank?	el banco?	el bahn-koh
the hotel?	el hotel?	el oh-tel
the post office?	la oficina de correos?	la oh-fee-see-nah deh-koh-reh-os
the museum?	el museo?	el moo-seh-oh
the hospital?	el hospital?	el ohss-pee-tal
the bathroom?	el baño?	el bahn-yoh
Here/there	Aquí/allá	ah-key/ah-yah
Open/closed	Abierto/cerrado	ah-bee-er-toh/ ser-ah-doh
Left/right	Izquierda/derecha	iss-key-er-dah/ dare-eh-chah
Straight ahead	Todo recto	toh-doh-rec-toh
Is it near/far?	¿Está cerca/lejos?	es-tah sehr-kah/ leh-hoss
I'd like . . .	Quisiera . . .	kee-see-ehr-ah
a room	una habitación	oo-nah ah-bee-tah-see-on
the key	la llave	lah yah-veh
a newspaper	un periódico	oon pehr-ee-oh-dee-koh
a stamp	un sello	say-oh
How much is this?	¿Cuánto cuesta?	kwahn-toh kwes-tah

A little/a lot	Un poquito/ mucho	oon poh-kee-toh/ moo-choh
More/less	Más/menos	mahss/men-ohss
I am ill	Estoy enfermo(a)	es-toy en-fehr-moh(mah)
Please call a doctor	Por favor llame un medico	pohr fah-vor ya-meh oon med-ee-koh
Help!	¡Ayuda!	ah-yoo-dah

On the Road

Avenue	Avenida	ah-ven-ee-dah
Broad, tree-lined boulevard	Paseo	pah-seh-oh
Highway	Carretera	car-reh-ter-ah
Port; mountain pass	Puerto	poo-ehr-toh
Street	Calle	cah-yeh
Waterfront promenade	Paseo marítimo	pah-seh-oh mahr-ee-tee-moh

In Town

Cathedral	Catedral	cah-teh-dral
Church	Iglesia	tem-plo/ee-glehs-see-ah
City hall, town hall	Ayuntamiento	ah-yoon-tah-me-yen-toh
Door, gate	Puerta	poo-ehr-tah
Main square	Plaza Mayor	plah-thah mah-yohr
Market	Mercado	mer-kah-doh
Neighborhood	Barrio	bahr-ree-o
Tavern, rustic restaurant	Mesón	meh-sohn
Traffic circle, roundabout	Glorieta	glor-ee-eh-tah
Wine cellar, wine bar, wine shop	Bodega	boh-deh-gah

Dining Out

A bottle of . . .	Una bottella de . . .	oo-nah bo-teh-yah deh
A glass of . . .	Un vaso de . . .	oon vah-so deh
Bill/check	La cuenta	lah kwen-tah
Breakfast	El desayuno	el deh-sah-yoon-oh
Dinner	La cena	lah seh-nah
Menu of the day	Menú del día	meh-noo del dee-ah
Fork	El tenedor	ehl ten-eh-dor
Is the tip included?	¿Está incluida la propina?	es-tah in-cloo-ee-dah lah pro-pee-nah
Knife	El cuchillo	el koo-chee-yo
Large portion of tapas	Ración	rah-see-ohn
Lunch	La comida	lah koh-mee-dah
Menu	La carta, el menú	lah cart-ah, el meh-noo
Napkin	La servilleta	lah sehr-vee-yet-ah
Please give me . . .	Por favor déme . . .	pohr fah-vor deh-meh
Spoon	Una cuchara	oo-nah koo-chah-rah

INDEX

FODOR'S POCKET MADRID

EDITORS: Carissa Bluestone, Christine Cipriani, Laura M. Kidder

Editorial Contributors: Mark Little, George Semler

Editorial Production: Marina Padakis

Maps: David Lindroth, *cartographer*; Bob Blake and Rebecca Baer, *map editors*

Design: Fabrizio La Rocca, *creative director*; Tigist Getachew, *art director*; Melanie Marin, *photo editor*

Production/Manufacturing: Angela L. McLean

Cover Photograph: Ricardo Ordoñez/Age Fotostock America

IMPORTANT TIP

Although all prices, opening times, and other details in this book are based on information supplied to us at press time, changes occur all the time in the travel world, and Fodor's cannot accept responsibility for facts that become outdated or for inadvertent errors or omissions. So **always confirm information when it matters,** especially if you're making a detour to visit a specific place.

SPECIAL SALES

Fodor's Travel Publications are available at special discounts for bulk purchases for sales promotions or premiums. Special editions, including personalized covers, excerpts of existing guides, and corporate imprints, can be created in large quantities for special needs. For more information, contact your local bookseller or write to Special Markets, Fodor's Travel Publications, 280 Park Avenue, New York, NY 10017. Inquiries from Canada should be directed to your local Canadian bookseller or sent to Random House of Canada, Ltd., Marketing Department, 2775 Matheson Boulevard East, Mississauga, Ontario L4W 4P7. Inquiries from the United Kingdom should be sent to Fodor's Travel Publications, 20 Vauxhall Bridge Road, London SW1V 2SA, England.

PRINTED IN THE UNITED STATES OF AMERICA

10 9 8 7 6 5 4 3 2 1